ON DISTANT SHORE

By Val G. Abelgas

Part 1

VAL G. ABELGAS

Publisher-Editor, Philippine Post

Editor, www.thepinoyweekly.com

Columnist, On Distant Shore

valabelgas@aol.com

ISBN - 13: 978 - 1976131837
ISBN - 10: 1976131839

Contact: job elizes@ yahoo.com
Website: http://tinyurl.com/mj76ccg

About the author

Val G. Abelgas, Publisher and Editor-in-Chief of the Los Angeles-based Philippine Post, has been a professional journalist for almost 45 years, 20 of them in Manila and 25 years in Los Angeles.

Val started as a sportswriter in the now defunct Philippine Daily Express in 1972 while still in his junior year in journalism at the University of the Philippines' Institute of Mass Communications. He rose to become city editor of then the country's biggest daily newspaper at a very young age of 24. He was the last managing editor of the Daily Express, which was closed down by the Cory Aquino administration in 1987. The next day, he moved to the Manila Standard as its first managing editor.

After stints as editorial consultant of the Philippine Star Group and later managing editor of the Philippine Times Journal, he and his family immigrated in 1991 to the United States, where he later obtained his green card as an alien of extraordinary ability in the field of journalism. In his first year in the US, he was editor of the Los Angeles Monitor and the next year became the first editor-in-chief of Balita. He moved to the Philippine Times in 1993, during which time he won the Newspaper of the Year and Columnist of the Year awards of the Philippine Press Club of America for two straight years in 1993 and 1994. In November 1993, he organized the first-ever nationwide convention of Filipino-American editors in Los Angeles with President Fidel V. Ramos as guest speaker. In 1995, he left the Philippine Times to join his wife Marisse in editing the Philippine Post and later became editor of Ang Peryodiko, the Pinoy Weekly and the Philippine Tribune. He published and edited two magazines with his wife, the Philippine Post Magazine and the Hiyas Magazine.

Before becoming a professional journalist, Abelgas was editor-in-chief of The Nucleus, official organ of the Manila Science High School, assistant news editor of the Philippine Collegian, official newspaper of the University of the Philippines, and editor-in-chief of the Campus Journal, laboratory newspaper of the UP-IMC.

Abelgas wrote a column, "As We See It," for the Philippines Daily Express in the 1980s. In 1992, he started writing his weekly "On Distant Shore" column, which is being published in 9 Filipino publications in the US and Canada.

Val has won numerous journalism awards both as a professional and campus journalist and served as director of the National Press Club of the Philippines five times and president of the Philippine Press Club of America. In 2016, he was named Journalist of the Year by the Filipino-American Press Club of California. He has travelled to more than 30 countries in official assignments as a journalist.

ooooo

Special Note

Articles are arranged in reversed chronology descending from newer dates to older dates

Contents

1

Secretary of Injustice
September 3, 2017

VITALIANO Aguirre II first hit the headlines in 2012 when, as one of the private prosecutors in the impeachment trial of Chief Justice Renato Corona, he covered his ears while the late Senator Miriam Defensor Santiago was scolding prosecutors for withdrawing the remaining articles of impeachment on the 26th day of the trial.

"You've been misleading the court! I'm very concerned that prosecution has been in bad faith all along. You've been saying to media, 'Panalo na kami.' Kami ang magdedesisyon niyan, hindi kayo. Ang yayabang niyo! Mga gago naman! (You are being conceited! Stupid!)" the feisty Santiago said in her speech.

After Sen. Jinggoy Estrada informed the body of Aguirre's "disrespectful" act, then Senate President Juan Ponce Enrile called for a recess, but Santiago continued to chastise Aguirre, who was later cited for contempt by the Senate, acting as an impeachment court.

Actually, Aguirre had not shied away from controversy even before that episode. The San Beda law class valedictorian was the lawyer for his classmate and fraternity brother, then Davao City Mayor Rodrigo Duterte, when then Commission on Human Rights Chair Leila de Lima was investigating the alleged Davao Death Squad.

Aguirre also represented retired police officer Bienvenido Laud, also known as "Tatay Laud," whom he defended up to the Supreme Court to try to block authorities from searching his quarry in Davao City, said to have been a burial ground of those supposedly killed by the DDS.

In 2009, De Lima, armed with a search warrant issued by a Manila judge, led a team that dug the quarry in search of evidence to claims by a self-confessed killer that he and six others were instructed by "Tatay Laud" to bring bodies of their victims to three caves in the quarry site. They were stopped by Aguirre, who argued before the Supreme Court that the search warrant was invalid as it was issued by a judge in Manila, who, he said, had no territorial jurisdiction. The digging had already yielded some leg bones, skull parts and some license plates.

The Supreme Court eventually ruled that the search warrant was valid after five years, in 2014, but no search was conducted again.

In 2016, after Duterte was proclaimed president-elect, Aguirre was among the first appointees to his Cabinet. In just the second month of his presidency, Duterte started the persecution of De Lima, alleging that De Lima had been having an affair with her driver, Ronnie Dayan, who Duterte also alleged functioned as De Lima's collector for drug protection money when she was the Justice secretary.

A few months later, De Lima was detained on drug-related charges for allegedly using her position as Secretary of Justice to acquire money from drug pushers inside the National Bilibid Prison to make their drug business operational even though they are imprisoned.

In all these cases against De Lima, Aguirre was in the forefront of her public persecution and prosecution, which was obviously in retaliation for her vociferous opposition of Duterte's brutal drug war and for her past investigation of the Davao Death Squad.

Shortly after De Lima's incarceration in February, Aguirre proved he was also an effective rabble-rouser when he spoke in a pro-Duterte rally and asked boastfully who the crowd wanted to be arrested next, to which the Duterte trolls shouted "Trillanes!" When questioned by senators on his highly partisan act, he said it was just a joke.

After revealing him as a jester cum justice secretary, Aguirre earned another title as the "Fake News King" after he stated that Vice President Leni Robredo stayed in the home of Fil-Am community leader Loida Nicolas-Lewis, who has been erroneously tagged by Duterte and Aguirre as the leader of a plot to oust the President. This was denied by both Robredo and Lewis.

In February after the abduction and killing of South Korean Jee Ick Joo allegedly by rogue policemen, Aguirre blamed the Korean Mafia, which, he said, has extended its reach to the Philippines. This claim was never proven nor followed up.

Later, he again proved he was worthy of the title "Fake News King" when he told reporters that the wife of one of the inmates who testified against De Lima was ambushed. Of course, it was not true, with no less than the Philippine National Police denying there was such an ambush.

At the height of the Marawi siege on June 7, Aguirre suggested dthat Senators Bam Aquino and Antonio Trillanes IV, and Magdalo Rep. Gary Alejano might be involved in the planning of the siege. Showing a picture of the three and Rolando Llamas, former political adviser of former President Noynoy Aquino, meeting with the heads of the prominent Lucman and Alonto families allegedly on May 2, the justice secretary said the Maute attack could be part of a destabilization plot against Duterte because, he said, two weeks after the alleged meeting, the siege started.

It turned out that the picture was from the Facebook wall of Zamboanga del Sur Vice Governor Ace Cerilles and was taken on Sept. 4, 2015 at the Iloilo International Airport. At the same time, Aquino, Trillanes and Alejano proved beyond reasonable doubt that they were not in Marawi on May 2 and were, in fact, in the capital attending congressional session.

Aguirre never apologized for the grievous error, saying he made it clear to the media that it was just a raw intelligence report, but the reporters protested and presented video recording of the press conference.

Trillanes commented: "The incompetence of Aguirre is only matched by his stupidity. I would advise him to avoid getting his intel from Facebook conspiracy theorists."

Like a troll, Aguirre has blindly defended Duterte's deadly drug war. After the killing of Albuera, Leyte Mayor Rolando Espinosa by policemen serving a search warrant in the wee hours of the morning inside the mayor's cell, Aguirre submitted a resolution downgrading from murder to homicide the charges against the policemen and Police Superintendent Marvin Marcos.

Sen. Franklin Drilon, the Senate minority leader and a former justice secretary, called the DOJ resolution an "insult to the Senate" and a "big blow to [the] justice system in the country." The Senate had recommended the filing of murder charges against Marcos and the other policemen in the Espinosa killing.

And then last week, amid widespread public outrage over the killing of 17-year-old Kian de los Santos, Aguirre sought to downplay the anger by describing Kian's death as "blown out of proportion" and "isolated."

Despite medical examiners' findings that Kian was kneeling and bent on the ground when shot at the back of the head and in the back, testimonies by eye witnesses, and footage from the barangay CCTV, Aguirre insisted that the witnesses who gave statements on what they saw during the alleged police operations that night had been polluted, or brainwashed by Senator Risa Hontiveros, who has courageously taken the cudgels for Kian's family.

Aguirre's repeated relaying of fake news and obvious partisan views got the attention of a group of young leaders that calls itself Millennials Against Dictators (MAD) who filed a formal complaint with the Ombudsman for Aguirre's alleged violation of the Code of Conduct and Ethical Standards for Public Officials and Employees. They called for the removal of Aguirre for spreading fake information while acting in his capacity as a Cabinet official.

"Respondent grossly neglected his duties and has made a mockery of the justice system where perceived foes are publicly persecuted rather than properly investigated and prosecuted," it said.

This is the same justice secretary who said that Duterte cannot be charged with crimes against humanity before the International Criminal Court because, according to him, criminals are not part of humanity.

He has been called a joker, the Fake News King, a rabble-rouser, and a fiesta barker. But based on the damage he has done as head of the Department of Justice, we can call him the Secretary of Injustice.

Ooooo

2
Let the bells ring
August 22, 2017

A DAY after Bulacan policemen killed 32 drug suspects in a single day, President Duterte commended them and told policemen all over the country to kill 32 more a day to reduce the country's drug problem.

"Yung namatay daw sa Bulacan, 32 in a massive raid. Maganda yun," the President said. "Pumatay tayo another 32 everyday, maybe we can reduce what ails this country."

The next day, Manila policemen killed 26 more drug suspects, and the following day, at least 18 more were gunned down by policemen in other places of the country. That brought a total of at least 76 killed in three days in the renewed drug war ordered by the President.

If 76 deaths in three days do not alarm the Filipino people, then that's another reason for the more rational and humane human beings to be concerned about. People like Vice President Leni Robredo and Sen. Francis Pangilinan have been lamenting the nonchalant attitude of Filipinos toward the more than 7,000 drug-related deaths recorded during the first year of President Duterte. Pangilinan said Filipinos should not remain mum in the face of these killings and asked if they still valued human life.

Pangilinan blamed the apathy among Filipinos in the drug deaths for the spate of political killings in the previous week that resulted in the murder of seven persons, including a judge and three media members, by motorcycle-riding men. None of the suspects in those murders have been arrested and police have instead resumed the drug war with even more intensity.

In that three-day renewed drug killings, a 17-year-old student was among those shot dead. While policemen in Ozamis City were careful to make sure the CCTVs around the house of Ozamis Mayor Reynaldo Pajorinog were not working on the night they raided the mayor's house and killed Pajorinog, his wife and 13 others, the Caloocan policemen were caught in the CCTV beating Kian Lloyd de los Santos, before the youth was allegedly given a gun, told to run and shot three times in the back and head.

Kian's death finally roused many people to the brutality of Duterte's drug war. Senators from both the ruling majority and the minority spoke as one to demand an investigation into Kian's death and a second look at the brutal drug war.

Ironically, it was Duterte's top ally in the Senate, Senate President Aquilino Pimentel III, who was the first to express alarm on the mounting death toll in the President's drug war.

Pimentel, finally finding the courage and wisdom of his venerable namesake father, welcomed his fellow senators' proposals to launch a new Senate investigation into the killings related to the government's anti-drug war, particularly on how the Philippine National Police (PNP) implements its anti-illegal drug campaign Oplan Double Barrel and whether it observes the standard operating procedures during operations.

Pimentel said the investigation should look into police claims that all those that have been killed engaged the police in a gunfight. Indeed, is it possible that the more than 7,000 killed in the drug war all fought back, many of them alleged to have grabbed a policeman's gun and fired at the policemen?

Commission on Human Rights Chairman Chito Gascon also called for an impartial investigation of the recent killings. "We need to make sure that our prosecutors do their job of investigating thoroughly all of these cases and filing appropriate charges. Otherwise, the climate of impunity… perpetuated and promoted by President Duterte will create the conditions of ratcheting up the body count," Gascon said.

Amnesty International, in condemning the latest drug deaths, said the Philippine government's bloody war on drugs was "plumbing new depths of barbarity." The human right watchdog called on the United Nations to investigate the deaths.

Even artists and celebrities joined in the condemnation. "We, Filipino cultural workers, condemn the killings wrought by the war on drugs, especially of the innocent, the young, and those caught in the crossfire," they said in a statement released on Sunday. "We denounce the normalization of these killings, the pardon of rogue police and military men, and the abetting of authorities' abuse against citizens."

The artists added: "Where Filipinos are dying on mere suspicion of involvement in drugs, where deaths are justified by victims' inclusion in questionable drug lists, where a few grams of drugs on a person has been used to justify murder, government has fallen silent on the P6.4-billion worth of smuggled drugs from China, for which there have been no suspects charged."

The critics have all pointed out that while police are quick to gun down small-time drug users and pushers, they have been cautious in arresting and filing cases against known bigtime drug lords, especially those who have been smuggling shabu through the country's ports. Instead of running after the drug lords, who are after all the perpetrators of the drug problem, the police, under the orders of the President, are basically shooting down the victims. And they think this would eliminate the drug problem and make the country move forward?

The Roman Catholic Church, led by its top two leaders, condemned the killings. Manila Archbishop, Cardinal Luis Tagle expressed concern about the increase in the number of deaths. "The illegal drug problem should not be reduced to a political or criminal issue. It is a humanitarian concern that affects all of us," Tagle said.

Lingayen-Dagupan Archbishop Socrates Villegas, president of the Catholic Bishops Conference of the Philippines, laments: "They say that if there are 32 killed every day, our lives would be better, and our countrymen nod in agreement. They applaud and cry with a smile… while counting corpses in the night, while passing wakes for the dead left and right."

"Don't we know how to weep? Why aren't we shocked by the gunfire and flow of blood on the sidewalk? Why aren't we angry at the flow of drugs from China? Why is it that it's only the poor who are shot while if a rich person with connections with higher ups is tagged, there needs to be an investigation and affidavit first," Villegas asked.

The UP Alpha Sigma Fraternity, to which this writer proudly belongs, put Kian's death in the proper perspective: "This story is a familiar one, one where the police fire on a helpless, scared individual and plant evidence on the dead body. It is a story that has been told time and time again by relatives of the victims of these anti-drug extrajudicial killings. It is a story that we have heard almost every day since the Filipino people decided to put a man who has shown little to no regard for the sanctity of human rights in charge of the country. It is a story of anti-poor policies, the abuse of power, and a culture of impunity and violence."

In essence, while he claims he wants to stop the country from becoming a narco-politico state, he is actually turning the Philippines into a fascist state where people get killed extra-judicially, where the rule of law is disregarded, where human rights are sacrificed in the name of peace and progress, and where critics are threatened with incarceration or death.

And how did Duterte react to all these protestations? While promising to jail the Caloocan policemen if found guilty (there's the big IF), Duterte said he was not backing down on his drug war, and again arrogantly dared his critics to oust him if they can.

In the face of this arrogance, people should also step up its protests until the Duterte administration finally realizes the futility of its brutal drug war. Archbishop Villegas called for churches in

Northern Luzon to ring their bells for 15 minutes starting at 8 p.m. from Aug. 22 to Nov. 27 as a prayer offering for the victims of the police operations in Pampanga province and Metro Manila last week and as a reminder to the living to stop supporting the killings.

I say let the bells ring until they rouse people from apathy and to the brutality of this drug war.

Ooooo

3

What about the bigger crimes?

August 10, 2017

THOUSANDS of suspected drug users and pushers have been killed since President Duterte launched his war on drugs last year and police officials, led by PNP chief Director General Ronald de la Rosa, are claiming that because of this ongoing drug war, there has been a noticeable drop in crimes in the country.

And yet, in a span of a few days last week, there have been seven cold-blooded murders and De la Rosa and his top officials have not found the same urgency that they had shown in enforcing Duterte's deadly drug war to go after the perpetrators of these murders. In fact, except for the usual "we will go after the killers" promised by the investigators, the President and his top cop De la Rosa have not said anything about the recent spate of killings.

The series of killings started on Thursday, August 3, when a motorcycle-riding tandem gunned down a former editor of Businessworld and his businessman brother inside their car in San Juan. The two gunmen fired a total of 34 bullets on Michael Marasigan, who is currently a public relations consultant for Finance Secretary Carlos Dominguez III and Davao Rep. Antonio Floirendo, and his brother, Christopher.

On Saturday, August 5, motorcycle-riding assailants gunned down a Pasay City councilor as he was emerging from a mall in Las Pinas. Councilor Borbie Rivera, who was also the president of Liga ng mga Barangay sa Pilipinas, was dead on arrival in the hospital with three gunshot wounds.

Earlier that day, Butuan Judge Godofredo Abul Jr. and his wife were shot dead by a lone gunman inside their garage as they were about to leave home in Butuan City. The gunman fled on a motorcycle driven by an accomplice. Abul was the second judge killed this year in Mindanao, which has been under martial law since May. The first one was retired Surigao City Judge Victor Canoy, who was also gunned down last February.

On Sunday, August 6, a radio broadcaster, Dahunan Alicaway, was shot and killed by two motorcycle-riding men while on his way home in Molave, Zamboanga del Sur also in Mindanao. The next day, Monday, another radio broadcaster Leodoro Diaz was gunned down by two motorcycle-riding men in Sultan Kudarat, also in Mindanao.

Last Wednesday, August 9, a lone gunman barged in a house in Batangas City where people were watching the Gilas-China basketball game on TV and shot tabloid columnist Cris Ibon and his driver. Ibon and the driver survived, but the latter was hit in the spine and could be paralyzed for life.

Sen. Francis Pangilinan, president of the opposition Liberal Party, blamed the culture of impunity spawned by Duterte's drug war for the string of killings, adding that such deaths arose from the apathetic attitude of many Filipinos toward the mounting number of drug-related killings in the past months.

Pangilinan said these killings were the result of the nonchalant attitude of Filipinos toward the more than 7,000 drug-related deaths recorded during the first year of President Duterte. Pangilinan said Filipinos should not remain mum in the face of these killings and asked if they still valued human life.

There have been so many murders committed through the years, many of them by these motorcycle-riding tandems, and most of them remain unsolved until now. Unless perhaps the PNP shifts its focus on going after these murderers on motorcycles and the people who hired them, we don't expect any of these latest killings to be solved.

The lack of political will on the part of our police and national leaders to go after the perpetrators of these murders, the slow grind of justice, and the government's inconsistent policy on human rights and crime prevention have contributed to the continuation of a culture of impunity in the country.

It may look silly, but the proposal of a Manila councilor to ban "riding in tandem" on motorcycles in the city is at least the first government action against crimes committed by these so-called "riding in tandem" murderers.

If our police and government leaders can come up with a list of drug users and drug lords in all barangays, which, according to the President, come close to 3 million all over the country, I can't see why they cannot identify a single one of these hired murderers and bring them to justice, or since the police can kill a lowly drug user whose only crime probably was that he harassed some neighbors while he was high on drugs, they should probably shift their "swift justice" in eliminating these hired guns.

The only problem with this is that if Duterte ordered policemen to shoot to kill these hired murderers, another 7,000 men in slippers would end up dead while the real killers and their masterminds would be laughing as they watch the events unfold. Just like many big drug lords continue to evade arrest, much less being left bloodied on city streets.

With the seven recent murders hogging the headlines the past week, it's time the police shift their attention from the deadly drug war to catching the perpetrators and masterminds of the hundreds of unsolved political and media killings and other high-profile murders.

But to the country's policemen, that's hard work. After all, identifying and killing the lowly drug user is much easier. And they get rewarded, too.

Ooooo

4

What happened to 'never again'?

July 29, 2017

WHAT ever happened to "Never again to martial law"? A phrase opt-repeated in many rallies long after the Filipino people ousted the dictatorship of the late Ferdinand Marcos in what is now known as "People Power," it seems "never again" has lost its luster in the face of the emergence of another strongman that doesn't hesitate to say Marcos was his idol.

President Rodrigo Duterte declared martial law in May throughout Mindanao to quell what he insisted was a rebellion by extremists who, he said, was planning to establish a caliphate in Marawi City, and it seemed the whimper of "never again" by a few souls were drowned out by the "ayes" of Duterte's bootlickers in the not-so-hallowed halls of Congress.

Instead of convening in joint session to debate on whether the martial law declaration was in accordance with the provision of the 1987 Constitution and whether "rebellion or invasion" actually existed in Mindanao, the House of Representatives and the Senate separately passed resolutions endorsing Proclamation 216 – the present-day equivalent of Marcos' infamous Proclamation 1018 – with not even a shadow of deliberation or discussion.

The Supreme Court, supposedly the people's last resort, also absconded its constitutional duty to review the martial law declaration when it ruled that it was not equipped with facts to conduct such review and basically left it to the President to make the determination by simply showing probable cause – not incontrovertible facts – that rebellion or invasion exists.

Only one justice dared mention that popular phrase "never again." In his dissenting opinion, Justice Marvic Leonen said: "Never again should this Court allow itself to step aside when the powerful invoke vogue powers that feed on fear but could potentially undermine our most cherished rights. Never again should we fall victim to a false narrative that a vague declaration of martial law is good for us no matter the circumstances. We have the courage to never again clothe authoritarianism in any disguise with the mantle of constitutionality."

Last Saturday, Congress met in a hurried joint session and with an overwhelming vote of 261-18, elected to extend – not for another 60 days – but for the rest of the year, exactly as requested by Duterte, throughout the region of Mindanao.

Did we expect more from a chamber whose leader has suggested that martial law should be extended until the end of Duterte's term in 2022?

Senators Risa Hontiveros and Franklin Drilon were allowed to raise questions to some members of Duterte's Cabinet, led by martial law administrator Defense Secretary Delfin Lorenzana during a supposed hearing, but for a few ramblings and unrelated facts, failed to answer the following questions:

• "Why is there a need to extend martial law until December if the government claims that it is in full control of the situation, that the skirmishes are confined to Marawi City and that most of the Maute have been "neutralized?"

• "What does the government hope to achieve by martial law that it cannot bring to pass by any of the laws now in force, such as the Human Security Act (the Anti-Terrorism Law)?"

Indeed, why extend martial law until December and throughout Mindanao, and not just in Marawi City when the government has repeatedly said that the rebellion has been contained? Lorenzana echoed what Duterte and Malacanang spokesmen have repeatedly said in justifying martial law in the region – that there is real danger that the rebellion could spread to other areas in Mindanao and such danger must be stopped now.

Even assuming that rebellion actually does exist in Marawi City because of the Maute Group, does the same situation exist outside Marawi? Apparently not, because Duterte and the military have never mentioned a similar rebellion in Davao, Sulu or any other place, except to say that there is imminent danger of the rebellion spreading to other areas in the region.

The 1987 Constitution precisely did away with the phrase "imminent danger thereof" in the 1935 Constitution to prevent a repeat of Marcos' martial law. The 1987 Constitution instead mandates that the President can only declare martial law if there is clear evidence that rebellion (or invasion) actually exists and that public safety demands it. Not just the fear of imminent danger of a rebellion or invasion.

If the proclamations of the military that only a handful of Maute members are in Marawi and that they are trapped in a small section of the city were true, will it take until December to vanquish them? What kind of military do we have then?

Speaker Pantaleon Alvarez and Presidential Spokesman Ernesto Abella said that martial law should be extended to eliminate once and for all the threat of extremism and insurgency in the region to enable Mindanao to grow to its potential. History tells us that military solution alone is not the answer to rebellion or insurgency, in the same manner that killing three million drug users will not solve the drug problem.

Marcos went all-out militarily against the Muslim and the communist insurgents throughout his 13-year martial rule but the Moro rebellion and communist insurgency both grew because the root problems that spawned them worsened. Government leaders will have to accept the fact that insurgency is directly proportional to poverty and injustice. As poverty and injustice grow, so does insurgency.

So why does Duterte, who has obviously religiously followed the life and work of Ferdinand Marcos, continue to believe that the only answer to the drug problem is killing the drug addicts, that the answer to insurgency is eliminating the insurgents, and that to curb criminality, criminals must be executed?

Why must a leader have emergency powers to solve nagging problems? For example, will giving him emergency powers, as proposed by his allies, solve the traffic problem, or the lack of infrastructure?

Is it democracy or the rule of law that is blocking progress for the Philippines, or the goal to eliminate poverty? Is Duterte conditioning our minds that martial law is the answer to all the country's problems? That achieving prosperity for the Filipino people is possible only under an atmosphere of fear and repression? That martial law is what the country needs?

No, please. Never again!

Ooooo

5

Clothing tyranny with constitutionality
July 10, 2017

WITH the Supreme Court basically showing reluctance to review President Duterte's martial law declaration and ceding its power to the President to determine the territorial scope of martial law, it now seems that the country's slide to tyranny is coming to near certainty.

Congress has earlier given up its power to review the bases for the martial law declaration by refusing to call for a joint session for a debate on the issue and instead voting to endorse the President's action without any discussion.

The high tribunal opted to ignore Duterte's threats to jail those who criticize or oppose his martial law declaration and his earlier defiant statement that he would listen only to the military on whether or not martial law should be lifted, and not to Congress or the Supreme Court.

The Supreme Court was oblivious to the authoritarian tendencies of the President as shown by his repeated warnings to the judiciary to stop issuing temporary restraining orders against government projects, his orders to policemen and the military to ignore the courts' orders against arresting suspects or searching homes without the proper warrants, his encouragements to policemen that have led to thousands of victims of extrajudicial killings, his repeated threats to the judiciary, the legislative and critics not to block his so-called reforms, and many more.

The capitulation of the Supreme Court, the people's last resort to uphold democracy and the rule of law, was evident in the martial law ruling. Instead of undertaking a thorough review of the factual bases of the martial law declaration over the entire Mindanao region, the Court, with the concurrence of 11 justices, ruled: "A review of the aforesaid facts similarly leads the Court to conclude that the President, in issuing Proclamation No. 216, had sufficient factual bases tending to show that actual rebellion exists."

The tribunal is mandated by the 1987 Constitution to undertake an impartial and through review of the factual bases for the martial law declaration, but it instead said it was not equipped with facts to conduct such review and basically left it to the President to make the determination by simply showing probable cause – not incontrovertible facts – that rebellion or invasion exists. Thus, its ruling: "After all, what the President needs to satisfy is only the standard of probable cause for a valid declaration of martial law and suspension of the privilege of the writ of habeas corpus."

The Supreme Court ruling also left the door open for the President to extend and expand his martial law declaration by saying: "Clearly, the power to determine the scope of territorial application belongs to the President… To reiterate, the Court is not equipped with the competence and logistical machinery to determine the strategical value of other places in the military's efforts to quell the rebellion and restore peace. It would be engaging in an act of adventurism if it dares to embark on a mission of deciphering the territorial metes and bounds of martial law."

This was also very evident when it said: "The Constitution grants him (the President) the prerogative whether to put the entire Philippines or any part thereof under martial law. There is no constitutional edict that martial law should be confined only in the particular place where the armed public uprising actually transpired. This is not only practical but also logical."

With only four justices expressing dissent, the Court basically abdicated its review powers over the declaration of martial law and the suspension of the writ of habeas corpus. What will stop President Duterte now to declare martial law all over the country when the police or the military claim that the Maute Group or the Abu Sayyaf or any other insurgent group has launched a rebellion in Bohol or in Quiapo? Duterte can claim that probable cause exists to declare martial law beyond Mindanao.

Congress – that renegade body of politicians – has shown it is subservient to its otherwise co-equal branch by refusing to perform its constitutional duty of calling for a joint session to discuss and to vote whether or not there was factual bases for the martial law declaration. In fact, the leader of the Lower House – clearly the inferior part of Congress – Speaker Pantaleon Alvarez has not only avidly defended the martial law declaration in Mindanao, but also openly pushes a five-year martial law period to last until the end of Duterte's term!

The same guy who has shown no respect for the Rule of Law when he threatened to jail and disbar three Court of Appeals justices for ordering the release of six Ilocos Norte officials being held hostage by the House of Representatives in its chambers, and who said he would tear up any Supreme Court ruling against martial law, now says the military needs five years to eliminate the threat of rebellion in Mindanao after his boss promised to remove the Maute Group from the bowels of the earth in 60 days.

Fortunately, the military leaders are not as kiss-ass as the country's congressional leaders and said a five-year martial law would be too long and that any extension beyond the 60 days allowed by the Constitution should be based on an "intelligent basis," meaning after a thorough examination of the actual field situation and its effects on the country and the population.

While I agree with the opinion of Associate Justice Antonio Carpio that martial law should have been declared only in Marawi City, where rebellion obviously exists, I must agree with the words of lone dissenter Justice Marvic Leonen when he warned against the Supreme Court repeating the same mistake when the tribunal legitimized President Marcos' martial law declaration in 1972 with only Justice Claudio Teehankee dissenting.

"Never again should this Court allow itself to step aside when the powerful invoke vogue powers that feed on fear but could potentially undermine our most cherished rights. Never again should we fall victim to a false narrative that a vague declaration of martial law is good for us no matter the circumstances. We have the courage to never again clothe authoritarianism in any disguise with the mantle of constitutionality," Leonen concluded in his 92-page dissenting opinion.

This was what the Supreme Court did in its favorable ruling – it clothed authoritarianism with the mantle of constitutionality.

Ooooo

6
Making health care unaffordable again
June 27, 2017

AFTER failing for many years to repeal the Affordable Care Act (ACA), popularly known as Obamacare, Republicans in both the House and the Senate are touting their control of Congress and are now ramming down a cruel legislation to finish a job they started just as soon as Obamacare became a law.

Speaker Paul Ryan and some Republicans accused the Democrats of rushing ACA through Congress. And yet, the House passed the American Health Care Act (AHCA), which would henceforth be known as the Trumpcare Bill, in a rush, without holding the prerequisite hearings and without waiting for an analysis by the non-partisan Congressional Budget Office.

The highly credible CBO later said in a report that the House bill would leave at least 23 million Americans uninsured in 10 years or by 2026. The report also confirmed one of the biggest worries of health-policy experts and constituents: that the bill could undermine protections for people with preexisting conditions.

Despite the unfavorable CBO report and surveys that showed only 16 percent of Americans support the House bill, the Senate Republicans, led by Majority Leader Mitch McConnell, announced an almost identical, nay worse, Senate version of the bill, and vowed to pass the legislation before the Fourth of July.

After weeks of meetings behind closed door, McConnell and company finally came up with a proposed Obamacare replacement that they now want to ram down Americans' throats without the benefit of thorough scrutiny and despite concerns raised, again, by the Congressional Budget Office.

The CBO said that the proposed Senate healthcare bill that would replace Obamacare would increase the number of Americans without health insurance by 2026 to 22 million, only one million short of CBO estimate of 23 million for the House version. The CBO report, which came a few days after McConnell announced the Senate version, said by next year alone, 15 million more Americans would be uninsured compared to the current law (ACA).

The CBO also said the Senate legislation would decrease federal deficits by a total of $321 billion over a decade, compared to $119 billion that the House version would do. Critics said these deficit reduction would result from cuts in federal subsidies to Medicaid, the federal-state program that provides insurance to about 70 million poor, disabled and elderly Americans; to special education programs; to programs that help people who do not get insurance through employers and have to buy their own policies; and to Planned Parenthood, which provides birth control, cancer screenings and other health services to 2.5 million people, mainly women.

In sum, the Republican-sponsored healthcare bills in both the House and the Senate would debilitate critical federal programs that provide health care to millions of Americans that could not otherwise afford to buy medical insurance. The Senate version would repeal most of the taxes imposed by the Affordable Care Act, including those on high-income people and on health care companies, to the detriment of the poor, disabled and the elderly.

Former President Barack Obama, the real target of President Donald Trump and his fellow hardcore Republicans in their obvious effort to reverse all of Obama's policies, slammed the Senate bill.

"The Senate bill, unveiled today, is not a health care bill," he wrote in a Facebook post. "It's a massive transfer of wealth from middle-class and poor families to the richest people in America. Simply put, if there's a chance you might get sick, get old, or start a family – this bill will do you harm. And small tweaks over the course of the next couple weeks, under the guise of making these bills easier to stomach, cannot change the fundamental meanness at the core of this legislation."

The Republicans have long wanted to repeal the Affordable Care Act, which is considered by many as Obama's most remarkable achievement, having provided insurance to 20 million previously uninsured Americans. They said Obamacare has caused insurance premiums to skyrocket and has deprived Americans of coverage in large swaths of the country and that their replacement bill would correct the flaws of Obamacare.

But the CBO and those in the know seem to believe otherwise. Even before the budget office released its report on Monday, the American Medical Association officially announced its opposition to the bill, and the National Governors Association urged the Senate to slow down.

McConnell wanted to force a vote on the Senate bill by last week but may be forced to delay the vote because of pressures from some Republicans. Five conservative Republican senators have said they cannot support the version of the bill and assuming all the Democrats and independents vote against it, only two negative Republican votes are enough to derail yet another move to repeal Obamacare.

"Currently, for a variety of reasons, we are not ready to vote for this bill, but we are open to negotiation and obtaining more information before it is brought to the floor," said four of the senators — Rand Paul of Kentucky, Mike Lee of Utah, Ron Johnson of Wisconsin, and Ted Cruz of Texas — in a joint statement. They said the draft bill would not repeal Obamacare and lower healthcare costs.

The fifth senator, Sen. Dean Heller of Nevada later said he is opposed to the Senate repeal bill in its current form. Heller raised concerns about the bill's phase-out of Medicaid's expansion.

Reforming Obamacare to make it more beneficial to more Americans is commendable, but repealing it just to spite Obama and making it worse for the millions of Americans who otherwise cannot afford to buy insurance is another thing. The way the Republicans are derailing Obamacare, the new version should be named Unaffordable Care Act. These efforts should be opposed by the American people. ooooo

7
The mighty Speaker
June 26, 2017

POWER corrupts. And absolute power corrupts absolutely. This tenet has never been more evident than in the recent actions by the House of Representatives led by its Speaker, Rep. Pantaleon Alvarez, who threatened to abolish the Court of Appeals because it ordered the House to release six officials of the Ilocos Norte provincial government, who were cited for contempt and detained inside the confines of the chamber.

The six senior Ilocos Norte officials were cited for contempt for failing to answer questions in connection with the House inquiry into the alleged misuse of tobacco funds in the province. Some of the provincial officials said they could not remember the transaction in question while some apparently gave answers that were not to the liking of House Majority Leader Rodolfo Farinas, a former Marcos ally who is now in a feud with the Marcoses in Ilocos Norte.

Farinas is in his last term as Ilocos congressman and is expected to challenge the Marcos anointed in the 2019 local elections. Gov. Imee Marcos is also in her last term as governor.

The six Ilocos officials went to the Court of Appeals and sought protection under the writ of habeas of corpus, which empowers the court to order an institution holding the petitioners to present them. The appellate court granted them the writ and ordered their provisional release on a P30,000 bail.

Alvarez, obviously blinded by his newfound power, went ballistic. Alvarez said he would defy the court and the House has not released the six as of this writing. Fariñas said the CA could not infringe on the constitutional power of Congress to cite errant resource persons for contempt.

Alvarez, mimicking the tough talk of his friend President Duterte, told reporters: "That's gross ignorance of the law. Mga gago yang tatlong justices na yan!" Alvarez said, referring to the justices who issued the order. In different interviews, Alvarez also called the three justices "idiots," "rotten," and "crazy." In debates and discourses, name-calling has been known to show signs of inferior argument or an inability to present solid arguments.

Two days later, Alvarez dropped another bomb on the appeals court, threatening to abolish the court or reducing its budget to one peso, which would effectively shut it down, and insisted that the court had no authority to compel the House to release the so-called "Ilocos Six."

"The CA is not even our co-equal branch. It is merely a creation of Congress. It exists because it was created by Congress," Alvarez told a radio interview. "The CA justices had better start thinking because any time, we can dissolve the CA." If this is not a threat, I don't know what is.

This is simply a case of bullying by the country's fourth highest ranking official, who has shown his brute arrogance in many instances in the past. When his girlfriend had a spat with the girlfriend of another congressman, fellow Davaoeño and former friend Rep. Tony Floirendo, Alvarez threatened to scrap the 40-year-old joint venture agreement between the Bureau of Corrections and the Floirendo-owned Tagum Agricultural Development Co., Inc.

Earlier, Alvarez threatened all members of the administration coalition to vote in favor of the death penalty bill or face expulsion from their committee chairmanship and memberships. Akong his victim was former President and now Pampanga Rep. Gloria Macapagal Arroyo who was stripped of her functions as a deputy speaker.

Just recently, Alvarez threatened to disobey the Supreme Court if if ordered a joint session of Congress to review Duterte's martial law declaration.

"They [the SC justices] do not have the right to dictate on Congress what we should do," he said, citing separation of powers among the three branches of government. "Punitin ko yan [I will tear it up]!" he said, if the tribunal makes such a decision. Preempting the President, Alvarez also said martial law should be extended until the end of Duterte's term in 2022.

Alvarez was echoing a similar threat by the President, who said: "Until the police and the Armed Forces say the Philippines is safe, this martial law will continue. I will not listen to others. The Supreme Court, Congress, they are not here." Malacanang spokesmen, however, again backtracked for Duterte, saying that the President would honor any SC decision on martial law.

Congress has used its power of the purse in the past to threaten agencies under the executive department, but this time Alvarez and Farinas are challenging a court order and are in clear defiance of the law. Rather than challenging the court order before the Supreme Court – if they really believe that the appeals court is abusing its authority – Alvarez and Farinas decided to use their vast legislative powers to compel the CA to reverse its order.

Still not content with threatening to abolish the second highest court of the land, the House dynamic duo decided they would move to disbar the three CA justices who issued the order. On Monday, Farinas said 180 members of the House of Representatives have signed a draft resolution asking the Supreme Court to disbar the three justices of the Court of Appeals' Special Fourth Division for "ignorance of the law and abuse of authority."

Albeit with questionable intent, Farinas has at least decided to go before the Supreme Court to settle the issue. The Constitution vests the courts the power to issue the writ of habeas corpus precisely to ensure that no government official or entity would abuse its authority to detain individuals. It is a vital element of democracy to check abuse by the people who wield power.

The appellate court was merely enforcing the Rule of Law, which ordains that, in the words of San Beda Graduate of School Law Dean Fr. Ranhilio Aquino, "when a citizen is detained, jailed or otherwise deprived of significant and fundamental liberties, he may turn to the courts and ask them to inquire into the legality of the power that restrains him."

The CA action should not be interpreted as an affront to Congress. The Constitution dictates that a court can order Congress or any instrumentality of government to present the petitioners and explain why they are being detained. Similarly, Congress can summon court officials to appear before its hearings or reduce the judiciary's budget if it feels that such funding is not merited. This is how democracy works.

Separation of powers was embedded in the Constitution to ensure that none of the three branches of government – the Executive, Legislative and Judiciary – would abuse their powers and are working within the bounds of the law and the Constitution.

Simply, it is dictated by the rule of law, of which our new set of leaders in both Malacanang and Congress seem to have shown disregard and disrespect. Without the rule of law, the country could easily slip to anarchy or tyranny. But being a lawyer, I'm sure Alvarez knows that.

Ooooo

8
Trump just wouldn't listen
June 13, 2017

IN AN apparent attempt to please his voter base, President Donald Trump pulled out the United States from the Paris Agreement on Climate Change and turned America from the leader of the free world to a potential pariah in the global community, particularly in the field of climate change.

Trump has been found lacking by many of his supporters in many of his campaign promises, and this time he was determined to please his shrinking stream of supporters, never mind what his action would do to the future of this country and that of the entire planet.

He has promised change and although he vows to "make America great again," with the changes he has been proposing, the only thing consistent with his proposed changes is that they all seek to reverse the policies and programs that former President Obama has instituted in his eight years in office.

In pursuit of his "America First" policy, he pulled out of the proposed Trans-Pacific Partnership (TPP) that would establish a free trade zone among 12 Pacific nations, threatened to pull out of the North America Free Trade Agreement (NAFTA) with neighbors Canada and Mexico, threatened to withdraw financial support to and refused to affirm the mutual defense provision of the North Atlantic Treaty Organization (NATO), and is considering reducing American commitment to the United Nations.

Foreign relations expert Max Boot wrote in a Los Angeles Times article that Trump's isolationist policy is actually a "me-first policy." Boot said Trump sees every international treaty as a racket and every alliance as a rip-off. "But by destroying the foundations of the international order that the U.S. built, he risks destroying the unprecedented power and wealth we have accumulated since 1945," Boot wrote.

He added: "If the U.S. pursues a "me first" policy, then every country in the world will do the same — and the result will be international lawlessness. Predatory states such as Iran, Russia and China will do well in the resulting chaos, while our allies — if we have any left — will suffer."

All Trump's moves, as pointed out by another political analyst, were meant to portray him as a leader who is "standing up for Americans against the world," which makes his comparisons with Philippine President Rodrigo Duterte even more compelling. Duterte has also questioned the effectivity of the UN, slammed the European Union, threatened to sever ties with the US, and in the firs month of his term, said his government would not honor the Paris Agreement for the very same reasons Trump opposed it.

Duterte called the landmark climate change accord "stupid" and "absurd" because, he said, it was unfair that developed nations who caused much of the current level of global warning would now want developing countries such as the Philippines to contain their carbon emissions to certain levels.

"We have not reached the age of industrialization. We're now going into it. But you are trying to stymie (our growth) with an agreement that says you can only go up to here," he continued. "That's stupid. I will not honor that."

When an unnamed ambassador reminded him that the Philippines was a signatory to the agreement, Duterte replied: "That was not my signature. It's not mine."

To his credit, Duterte eventually listened to reason, signed the agreement and sent the document to the Senate last March, which ratified it unanimously within a few days, preventing the Philippines from becoming one of only three nations to reject the Paris accord, which has been signed and ratified by 195 nations, which all agreed to curb greenhouse gas emissions to limit the impact of global change on the planet.

The only two other countries to reject it are Nicaragua, which wanted a stronger commitment to curb carbon emissions, and Syria, which is torn by civil strife and couldn't worry about climate change at this time.

And now, the United States, which accounts for about 14 percent of global greenhouse gas emissions next only to China's 30 percent, has become the third nation to refuse to cooperate with the entire world to save the planet and make it more livable for future generations. Based on cumulative emissions since 1850, the United States is first with 29 percent of the total, then the EU with 27 percent, and finally China and Russia with eight percent each.

These science facts make it even more compelling for the United States to take the responsibility to lead, or at least join the global movement to curb carbon emissions and slow down global warming.

In rejecting the agreement, Trump said: "The Paris climate accord is simply the latest example of Washington entering into an agreement that disadvantages the United States to the exclusive benefit of other countries, leaving American workers…and taxpayers to absorb the cost in terms of lost jobs, lower wages, shuttered factories, and vastly diminished economic production."

But economists and political analysts said that leaving the accord will neither bring back jobs nor help the taxpayer, but will instead hurt the United States and the world.

Trump insists, as he had declared of other treaties, trade agreements and alliances from which he has or has threatened to pull out, that the Paris accord is unfair to the US. Political observers point out that the agreement is non-binding and that each signatory country is allowed to determine its own target level of reduction in carbon emissions. How can it be unfair?

Instead of totally withdrawing from the accord, all Trump had to do was reduce the target set by Obama, who pledged to cut carbon emissions in the US by 26 to 28 percent from 2005 levels by 2025. In fact, Trump had already started the process of reducing this target through an executive order he signed in March, which according to a study, would lower the reductions to just 15 to 19 percent from the 2005 levels by 2025. Why pull out from the accord then?

Trump claims that Americans have lost jobs and the US economy has suffered because of stringent environmental regulations over the past years. But economic data have shown that in the past several years the coal mining industry has created only 70 jobs compared to, for example, the solar energy sector which now employs twice as much as the coal industry. On the contrary, the renewable energy sector has been seen as a major contributor to the US economy.

Trump said he had to withdraw from the Paris accord "in order to fulfill my solemn duty to protect America and its citizens." But the President was only protecting the interest of a few coal miners that, like him, blame what US Environmental Protection Agency chief Scott Pruit ironically calls "climate exaggerators."

Trump can't claim to protect the interest of the American people because, unlike him who said during the campaign that climate change was a hoax, according to a Gallup poll nearly two-thirds of Americans are worried about climate change and according to the Yale Program on Climate Change Communication, almost 70 percent of Americans wanted to stay in the agreement, including half of Trump voters.

Big businesses affected by carbon emission reductions, including PG&E, National Grid, Chevron, ConocoPhillips, Exxon-Mobil, BP, Shell, General Motors, General Electric and even some of the largest coal producers, such as Arch Coal, Cloud Peak Energy, and Peabody Energy, informed the president that they wanted the United States to stay in the agreement. But he just wouldn't listen.

Almost everybody who were affected by recent weather disturbances all over the world are one in saying they have not experienced such storms and blizzards in years, and yet some are unable to relate these to global warming.

In March 2009, the world's foremost experts on global warming gathered in an emergency meeting in Copenhagen to warn politicians to act now to minimize the impact of what they described could be 'irreversible' climate shifts and hopefully save a world that they said was "on the brink."

The scientists were concerned that any significant delay in reducing emissions would lead to "a range of tipping points" that would make it significantly more difficult to reduce greenhouse gas levels.

The 2,500 scientists from 80 countries who attended the conference warned in their statement: "There is no excuse for inaction."

Trump just wouldn't listen.

Ooooo

9

Tyranny: The signs are clear
June 1, 2017

FOR THE umpteenth time, Malacanang spokesmen had to explain and tone down what President Duterte had casually told soldiers just a few days after declaring martial law in Mindanao. The President said he would ignore the Supreme Court and Congress if they meddled with his decision to declare martial law in Mindanao.

"Until the police and the Armed Forces say the Philippines is safe, this martial law will continue. I will not listen to others. The Supreme Court, Congress, they are not here," Duterte told soldiers on Saturday. "Are they the ones dying and losing blood, bleeding, hemorrhaging because there is no help, no reinforcement? It's not them."

As he usually does, he uses drama and bravado to gain the support of the people and his listeners, ignoring the fact that under the 1987 Constitution, which was promulgated exactly to prevent the repeat of the abuses under President Marcos' martial law, Congress and the Supreme Court have oversight powers in the event of a declaration of martial law.

The Constitution requires Congress to approve a president's declaration of martial law, and limits military rule for 60 days. If a president wants to extend it, he or she must again get congressional endorsement. The Supreme Court can also rule on martial law's legality and being the final arbiter on matters of law and constitutionality, its word is supposed to be final.

In Duterte's above remarks alone, he had already made known his intention to disregard the Constitution in: first, the oversight powers of the Supreme Court and Congress; and second, on the duration of martial law which he said would continue until the Armed Forces and the National Police tell him the country is safe. He even intimidated that martial law could last for one year.

The next day, Presidential Spokesman Ernesto Abella, obviously realizing that his boss had shot himself on the foot again, said Duterte had no intention of bypassing Congress and the Supreme Court on his martial law declaration.

"It simply means to say that those who have true and accurate report — and true and accurate report — in which he will depend on will be the military and the Philippine National Police," he said. But will he acquiesce to the high court or Congress if the two co-equal branches say enough of martial law? Not from the tone of Duterte's remarks nor from Abella's doublespeak.

During the same speech, Duterte said soldiers and policemen could conduct searches and make arrests without warrants from the court. He said they only need to get a signed arrest, search and seizure order (ASSO) from their commanders. But these ASSOs were precisely the document used by soldiers during martial law to commit abuses against civilians.

Besides, the 1987 Constitution is very clear that civil courts would continue to be open and that no arrests or searches can be made without warrants issued by these civilian courts.

Duterte also said his martial law would be harsh, just as Marcos' was, again ignoring provisions of the 1987 Constitution that ensure no abuses would be committed during the imposition of martial law.

The 1987 Constitution provides that even during martial law, the Bill of Rights must be strictly followed, civilian courts shall reign supreme, and the legislature cannot be abolished. The Charter is also very clear in ensuring that Congress and the Supreme Court must review the proclamation of martial law, whether it's justified and whether it conforms with the provision that martial law may only be declared in case of "invasion and rebellion."

Because its leaders and members are mostly loyal allies of the President, it seems Congress, especially the House of Representatives, is abandoning its duty and responsibility to review Duterte's martial law declaration. Speaker Pantaleon Alvarez and House Majority Leader Rudy Farinas, both avid Duterte loyalists, insist there is no need for a joint session to review the declaration when the Constitution is very explicit about the need for the Senate and the House to convene in joint session within 24 hours after receiving the President's report to deliberate on the martial law declaration and vote whether to allow it or not.

One question that the senators and congressmen have to discuss is whether the condition of "invasion and rebellion" exists, and if, indeed, such condition exists, does it merit a martial law declaration throughout Mindanao, and not just in Marawi City.

The opposition, led by Sen. Francis Pangilinan, filed a resolution calling for both houses to convene in a joint session for the sole purpose of reviewing the martial law declaration but being severely outnumbered, they have been ignored.

The Supreme Court has ruled in the 2012 case Colmenares vs. Arroyo that the review is automatic and not optional, and yet the Duterte boys in both the Senate and the House, unfortunately including Senate President Koko Pimentel, son of the venerable democratic icon Nene Pimentel, would rather ignore this than earn the ire of their leader.

Despite the doublespeak by his spokesmen, Duterte has long established by his actions and remarks that he is leading the country to the road to tyranny. Even during the campaign, he had threatened to abolish Congress if it blocked his agenda for reforms. He has shown a penchant for disregarding the rule of law as shown in his deadly drug war wherein he basically encouraged policemen to defy the law by promising to pardon them in case they were convicted in the performance of their duty.

He has shown a disdain for criticism, which is an important element in a democracy. He has jailed his foremost critic, Sen Leila de Lima, and is now threatening to do the same to Sen. Antonio Trillanes IV and other opposition politicians by using convicted criminals and the alleged pork scam mastermind to go against them.

He has threatened the judiciary many times, saying the courts are blocking his programs by issuing temporary restraining orders (TROs). He has warned the Supreme Court, a co-equal branch, not to bring the country into a constitutional crisis when it is he who has shown disrespect for the fundamental law of the land.

He has shown an utter disregard for human rights, as he justifies the killing and arrest without warrants of drug suspects to eliminate the country's drug problem.

The signs are there and are happening right before our very eyes – the Machiavellian principle of the end justifies the means, sacrificing human rights for the safety of the people or the common good, mass following of blind supporters who are willing to give him the blanket authority to do whatever he thinks is for the common good, government officials blindly defending the breakdown of the rule of law and disrespect for human life, a 91-percent rating that nurtured a leader's ego making him believe he is larger than life, labeling critics as stupid, idiot and immoral, muzzling media, and a feckless opposition. These are troubling and clear signs that we are on a "slippery slope to tyranny." It is up to Congress, the Supreme Court and a vigilant citizenry whether they would allow the democracy that the Filipino people fought valiantly for in 1986 to slip again from their grasp.

Ooooo

10
Playing with fire
May 25, 2017

THE rejection of $280 million in grants from the European Union last week and the visits of President Duterte to China and Russia in a two-week span validated what has become obvious since the former Davao City mayor became president in July last year – that the country is taking a 180-degree turn in its foreign policy.

Duterte, his spokesmen, and newly confirmed Foreign Secretary Alan Peter Cayetano describe these recent developments as the pursuit of an "independent foreign policy."

"We will not accept aid from any country if there are strings attached, if there are conditions, because we are an independent nation, and we have an independent foreign policy," Cayetano explained an earlier announcement by Malacanang that the Philippines would not accept grants from the EU "that may allow it to interfere with internal policies of the Philippines."

And yet, a few days earlier, Duterte proudly announced that he has received over $1 billion in pledges of official development aid from China where he had just attended the One Belt, One Road Summit along with 30 other heads of state. Both Duterte and Cayetano insist the China aid and grants had no conditionalities, in other words, "no strings attached."

The next day after rejecting the EU aid, Duterte flew to Russia, another newfound friend, where he expects to get hundreds of million dollars more in aid, including financial assistance that would help modernize the Philippine military. Again, I'm certain they would say, "no strings attached."

Either Duterte and his officials are too naïve, or they are lying through their teeth each time they say that Chinese and Russian aid, unlike those of the European Union and the United States, have no strings attached.

For example, China has offered a $500-million soft loan for the military, but the funds, as emphasized by Defense Secretary Delfin Lorenzana, would be used to purchase arms from China, not from any other country. Of course, any military aid from Russia would also have to be used to purchase weapons from Russia. In the same manner, the grants and loans pledged by China for infrastructure projects would have certain conditions, such as the inclusion of some Chinese contractors and suppliers.

But these are just the economic conditions of the grants. The more telling and critical conditions are those that pertain to what former Social Economic Planning Secretary Solita Monsod as the "policy conditionalities"—good governance, anti-corruption and the rule of law. Most of these conditions are imposed by donor countries from the West, such as the United States and European countries.

For example, foreign aids granted by the US-based Millennium Challenge Corporation are monitored to ensure that there is no corruption involved, and that there is a policy of good governance, the rule of law and respect for human rights in the country receiving aid. The same is true with grants and loans from World Bank, IMF, Japan ODA, and, of course, the European Union.

This, obviously, is the part that the Duterte administration resents and the reason it cites for rejecting the EU aid – what Presidential Spokeman Ernesto Abella calls "interfering with the country's internal affairs."

The rule of law and respect for human rights are two phrases that create a hurtful sting to Duterte's ears. He has called critics of his deadly drug war all sorts of names – "idiot," "stupid," "son of _ _ _ _ _ _ _," and many other expletives – and, in fact, in his latest tirade threatened to behead all human rights activists who dare criticize his war on drugs that has resulted in the death of more than 7,000 drug users and pushers.

Although he is a self-proclaimed leftist and a longtime hater of the United States, it is actually the concerns raised by the State Department, President Obama, the United Nations and the European Union on his war on drugs that triggered and fortified his policy of distancing the country from the Western allies and embracing his newfound friends China and Russia, which have not criticized his deadly drug war nor his disdain for the rule of law and human rights. After all, these two countries have totalitarian governments that respect neither the rule of law or human rights. It's a foreign policy Duterte and Cayetano conveniently call "an independent foreign policy."

But we all know that these two regional powers wouldn't give without getting much, much more in return. For example, China has been raping Philippine sovereignty in the South China Sea but since it is offering money that is hard to refuse, Duterte has opted to spread the country's legs and to enjoy the rape.

We do not question the President's sincerity in his desire to accelerate economic growth through infrastructure projects that China had pledged to finance, but has the Cabinet studied deeply and thoroughly the impact of the turnaround in foreign policy in the long term? Have they considered the pulse of the people in this foreign policy change? For example, a recent Pulse Asia survey showed that the countries least likely trusted by Filipinos are China and Russia, and the most trusted are the United States, Japan, Australia and Great Britain.

While Duterte and Cayetano are calling the foreign policy shift as an "independent foreign policy," experts are calling it a "hedging strategy," which a scholar has defined as "an insurance-seeking behavior under high-stakes and high-uncertainty situations, where a sovereign actor pursues a bundle of opposite and deliberately ambiguous policies vis-à-vis competing powers to prepare a fallback position should circumstances change."

This explains why the Duterte administration continues to hold Balikatan exercises with the US, to insist that the Mutual Defense Treaty and EDCA remain in force, while agreeing to hold joint military exercises with both China and Russia, and while playing footsies with America's adversaries.

The objective of this approach, according to an analyst at the National Defense College of the Philippines, is to "acquire as many returns from different powers as possible… while simultaneously seeking to offset longer-term risks."

Evidently, Duterte is trying to play the world's major powers, hoping to gain as much economic returns as the country could possibly get from them. Even on the matter of EU aid, Malacanang says it is still open to receiving grants from the European Union, which by the way is the Philippines' fourth largest trading partner, as long as they do not interfere with the country's internal affairs, meaning the EU should shut up with its criticism of Duterte's deadly drug war, disrespect for the rule of law and disregard for human rights.

In his desire to squeeze the maximum financial benefits from these major powers, the country could get caught in a situation it would have no control over. For example, in exchange for $1-billion pledges from China, Duterte has virtually abandoned the country's legitimate claim to the disputed islands in the South China Sea, a claim legally validated by an Internal Arbitrarial Court ruling. A few years from now, with Chinese military bases fortified on these islets, with the country becoming fully dependent on Chinese alms, and with ties with the US irreversibly cut off, it would be even more difficult for the Philippines to defend its sovereignty.

Playing the major powers is like playing with fire; it can burn you in the end.

Ooooo

11
Napoles should not be spared
May 16, 2017

THE tradeoff looks rather obvious. After Solicitor General Jose Calida appealed to the Court of Appeals to overturn the conviction of alleged pork barrel scam mastermind Janet Lim Napoles in January, the appellate court suddenly found no evidence establishing beyond reasonable doubt that Napoles abducted and kept hostage her cousin, Benhur Luy, and acquitted her.

That same day, both Calida and Justice Secretary Vitaliano Aguirre III said they were considering making Napoles a state witness in the numerous plunder cases filed in relation to the P10-billion peso pork barrel scam involving mostly ghost projects.

Many observers were surprised, nay shocked, when from out of the blue, Calida, the government's top lawyer who was supposed to lead in prosecuting Napoles for plunder, filed a manifestation before the Court of Appeals – just six months into the administration of President Duterte — recommending the acquittal of Napoles for the crime of serious illegal detention of Luy, who happens to be the whistle-blower and top prosecution witness in the plunder cases against Napoles, three senators and many other elected and appointed officials.

Why the Office of the Solicitor General would file such a manifestation was difficult to comprehend even for top legal experts. But five legal experts interviewed by the Philippine Center for Investigative Journalism (PCIJ) agreed that the OSG's manifestation signals "a policy shift in how the Duterte administration wants to deal with Napoles, Luy, other state witnesses and the lawmakers who had been indicted in the plunder cases involving the misuse of pork barrel funds now pending trial before the Sandiganbayan."

They described the move of the OSG under Duterte as "dangerous," "alarming" and "shocking."

Napoles had been sentenced by Makati Judge Elmo Alameda on April 14, 2015 to life in jail after a two-year trial. Napoles appealed to the Court of Appeals on Sept. 20, 2016, and just four months later, the OSG filed its manifestation recommending her acquittal. And less than four months later, the appellate court did just that.

The PCIJ report also noted: "Interestingly, just weeks before Napoles' lawyers filed her "reply brief" in September 2016, President Duterte himself had brought up the notorious businesswoman's case at a press conference in Davao City."

Duterte was quoted as having said that the Napoles case should be revisited. "The Napoles case should deserve a second look," Duterte said, "for it also involves corruption and (Senator Leila) de Lima." Hmmm, interesting.

The President's mention of De Lima as a target for the Napoles case revisit casts doubt on his sincerity in going after all those involved in the pork barrel scam. Many suspect with good reason that Napoles would be used to go after De Lima and other leading members of the opposition Liberal Party.

De Lima had said in the past that she rejected Napoles as a state witness because when asked by DOJ investigators to name the legislators involved in the pork scam, Napoles asked them instead who among the senators and congressmen did they want included in the list.

How can the prosecutors depend on a woman who is obviously willing to make false testimony to save her own skin? How can the judge believe a woman who boasted to her associates that as long as there is government, there is money to be made?

But De Lima herself had suggested twice in 2014 that Napoles could be a state witness. She said that between Gigi Reyes and Napoles turning state witness, she'd rather take Napoles because she would be able to name all the legsilators and officials involved in the scam. In August 2013, De Lima said she would not rule out tapping Napoles as a state witness, even though the law requires a state witness to be "not the most guilty of the crime charged."

Of course, former Senators Juan Ponce Enrile, Jinggoy Estrada and Bong Revilla are big fishes and could be as guilty as Napoles in the shameless scheme. But Napoles, being the alleged mastermind and the biggest beneficiary of the fraud, is the biggest fish of all because she was reportedly involved in all transactions dating to the time of Gloria Macapagal Arroyo.

It's like asking gang boss Al Capone to testify as state witness to bring all the politicians and policemen under his payroll to jail. It seems that Calida, Aguirre and Duterte would rather let go of the big fish, the alleged mastermind in the P10-billion pork barrel scam and the P900-million Malampaya fund mess, to go scot-free as long as she is able to jail the senators, lawmakers and other leaders of the opposition. Just like what then President Noynoy Aquino did to persecute Enrile, Estrada and Revilla, who were stalwarts of the then opposition party.

By all accounts, the 10 or so whistleblowers have made or submitted all testimonial and documentary evidence to prove beyond reasonable doubt that Napoles, several congressmen and senators, and several bureaucrats conspired to rob the people of more than P10 billion in government funds through an elaborate scam that involved huge kickbacks, ghost projects, fake or fraudulent NGOs, forgery, and bribery.

What can Napoles contribute that his former workers and close confidantes, who handled all the transactions, handed over cash, and forged several signatures, have not already revealed or have documentary proofs of?

As the alleged mastermind and biggest beneficiary, Napoles could be considered among the worst abusers of the system and justice requires that she be treated as defendant, not as state witness.

Letting the biggest fish off the hook to get at Duterte's worst critics is wrong, and smacks of selective justice! Making Napoles state witness and allowing her to go scot-free would only repeat the same errors and selective justice committed by the previous administration.

All that took part in that shameless scam should all go to jail, whether they are senators, congressmen, small and big bureaucrats, big or small contractors, and whether they are friendly to or critical of the administration. And that includes Janet Lim Napoles.

Ooooo

12
Deadly drug war doesn't work
May 13, 2017

IN September last year, President Duterte sent PNP chief Director General Ronald de la Rosa to Colombia to see "how they won the war on drugs." Apparently, De la Rosa wasn't listening or simply ignored what the Colombian officials said because months after that trip, the deaths in the administration's war on drugs continue to mount.

In April 2016, Colombian President Juan Manuel Santos told the United Nations that there should be a "more effective, lasting and human solution" to the problem that would address the issue at the root causes, and expand the fight beyond enforcement. Colombia had abandoned a deadly drug war initiated by then President Cesar Gaviria in the early 1990s that resulted, according to Gaviria himself, in the killing of tens of thousands of drug users and pushers in Colombia.

In an opinion piece in the New York Times, Gaviria, who is now part of the Global Commission on Drug Policy, said he "learned the hard way" that using force in fighting the war on drugs does not work.

"Illegal drugs are a matter of national security, but the war against them cannot be won by armed forces and law enforcement agencies alone," he said, adding that instead of containing Colombia's drug problem, it only worsened and created new problems.

"The war on drugs is essentially a war on people," he said, adding that there needs to be "an honest conversation," to get the drug menace under control. Gaviria wrote that President Rodrigo Duterte should learn from Colombia's experience that a drug war solely reliant on police and military might is "unwinnable."

But Duterte wouldn't listen. Instead, the tough-talking President called the former Colombian president an "idiot" for "lecturing" him on the war on drugs. Duterte said that the situations in Colombia and the Philippines are different because of the kind of illegal drugs trafficked in those countries, saying that in the South American nation, cocaine was the most prevalently used while in the Philippines, it is shabu or methampethamine, which he said uses a chemical used in manufacturing batteries.

"The fact alone that it is mixed using battery water will give you an indication of what's going to happen inside your brain," Duterte said. Whether there is truth to what he said has never been discussed.

Last week during a policy forum on drugs held at the University of the Philippines, five international experts in drug policy spoke out against the use of force and suggested that there are better ways than waging war against the users.

Agnes Callamard, United Nations special rapporteur who was the keynote speaker, said world leaders have already recognized that the war on drugs "does not work," and that many harms associated with narcotics were not caused by it but by "badly thought out policies."

She said ill-conceived policies not only fail to address drug abuse and trafficking but also "foster a regime of impunity infecting the whole justice sector and reaching into whole societies, invigorating the rule of violence rather than law," the UN special rapporteur on extrajudicial, summary and arbitrary executions said. She added that it also compounds problems such as extrajudicial killings; the breakdown of the rule of law; vigilante crimes, torture, ill-treatment and sexual violence; and detention in rehabilitation centers without trial, among others.

Callamard added that instead of a violent response to illegal drugs, heads of state are calling for a balanced, multifaceted and multidisciplinary approach that puts emphasis on health, rights and justice.

Carl Hart, neuro-psycho-pharmacologist from Columbia University, said wars against illegal drugs are actually campaigns against the poor and the undesired in society.

"All you need to do is to look at who is being arrested, who is being killed and what you will find is that it is the undesired people in your society, the poor people in your society. So in effect, it becomes a war on those undesirable."

Pascal Tanguay, who spoke on the experience of Thailand in its war on drugs, said the International Drug Policy Consortium has come up with different alternatives that can be implemented to address drug proliferation, including diversion, scaling of drug reduction, and evidence-based drug dependence treatment. "Essentially none of these are being implemented in the Philippines," he said.

John Collins, director of the International Drug Policy Program of the London School of Economics, also noted that the drug prevalence in the Philippines is lower than the global average, contradicting Duterte's claim that the country has become a narco-state.

He said that the Philippine government is acting on the wrong perception that it has reached a crisis point and there has to be severe action. Based on data, the Philippines is probably below average in terms of consumption rate on the international scale, Collins said.

Collins concluded: "Like any other development policy, you focus on the sustainable development goals, you focus on the basic principles of improving health and welfare, improving security, improving governance, improving democratic values, improving the rule of law. None of those things are assisted by the war on drugs."

The fifth speaker, Dangerous Drugs Board chairman Benjamin Reyes said the agency is set to submit to Malacañang a revised version of the Philippine Anti-Illegal Drug Strategy. The new strategy, he said, would be aligned with the priorities of the administration.

Reyes said the new policy would incorporate available principles and tools provided by prevention science and latest evidence-based treatments.

But it seems all their observations would again fall on deaf ears. Presidential chief legal adviser Salvador Panelo merely said the remarks of Callamard were based on hearsay, instead of saying that the government would look into their suggestions and see if they could be incorporated into the government efforts against illegal drugs.

Duterte should stop being too sensitive to criticisms, especially from these experts who have been studying the problem for many years now. It's time he abandons the deadly war on drugs and change his strategy in dealing with the problem. And then he can start focusing on battling the bigger problem of poverty, which after all is the root cause of the drug and other problems in the country.

Ooooo

13

Of secret cells and impunity
May 2, 2017

APPARENTLY, the Manila police station chief who detained 12 men and women inside a tiny secret cell was just following what appears to be the policy of the Duterte administration on drug pushers and users. Justice Secretary Vitaliano Aguirre III once said in defense of President Duterte's brutal drug war that the killing of the drug addicts did not constitute a crime against humanity because they "were not part of humanity."

And so, policemen all over the country, including Superintendent Robert Domingo of Manila Police Station 1 in Tondo, felt it was okay to treat drug suspects as animals – slaughtering them in the middle of the night, pulling them away from their homes without the benefit of arrest warrants, putting them in overcrowded jails, and squeezing them into a hidden cell so tiny they couldn't afford the luxury of lying down to sleep or rest, and so filthy they had to live beside their feces and urine.

This statement by Aguirre and repeated encouragement by the President himself that policemen – and even civilians – can go ahead and kill drug suspects if they resisted arrest have obviously been seen by the policemen as a go signal to do as they please with regards the alleged drug suspects. The President promised to defend the policemen and to pardon them if convicted of murder, again emboldening these crooks in uniform to do as they please.

After more than 7,000 deaths, not a single one has been investigated, or if investigated, has not resulted in any arrest of the killers. This and the irresponsible statements by Duterte and Aguirre have contributed to the worsening of the culture of impunity in the country.

So, it was not a surprise when Duterte's most avid henchman, PNP chief General Ronald "Bato" de la Rosa defended the Tondo police chief and personnel who have been accused of wrongful detention and of extorting money from the arrested drug suspects.

"As long as they haven't hurt or extorted from the detainees, it's OK with me," Dela Rosa said. The

PNP chief even questioned the timing of the raid by the Commission on Human Rights (CHR), saying it was meant to embarrass the administration at a time it was hosting the ASEAN Summit.

But, General de la Rosa, sir, that was precisely the complaints of the detained drug suspects – that they were tortured, made to endure subhuman conditions, and asked to fork from P40,000 to P200,000 for their release. How about investigating the complaints before even defending your personnel?

De la Rosa's defense of the Tondo policemen came just a day after the Manila police chief relieved the Tondo station chief and 12 other policemen, and thanked the CHR for exposing the existence of the secret cell. Director Oscar Albayalde of the National Capitol Region PNP thanked the CHR "for taking time" to inspect police stations and providing "an eye-opener for all of us to revisit the need for better detention cells and improvement of our jail facilities."

Obviously, Albayalde knows that the mere existence of a secret cell was illegal under the country's anti-torture laws. In fact, it is prohibited under the 1987 Constitution's Bill of Rights, as pointed out by lawyers belonging to the Center for International Law.

"Under our Constitution's Bill of Rights, "secret detention places, solitary, incommunicado, or other similar forms of detention are prohibited," they said. "The UN Convention on Torture (1986) and its Optional Protocol (2012), to which the Philippines is a party, also prohibit such secret detention cells."

When confronted by the CHR about the existence of a secret cell in the station, Superintendent Domingo first denied its existence.

But when the CHR raiders, accompanied by media, heard a woman's voice behind the wall and found a secret latch that revealed the tiny cell that held the 12 men and women, Domingo said they were just trying to maximize space.

The CHR also found no record of the dozen's arrest. When confronted by the CHR about this violation, Domingo again lied by saying that they had just been arrested and that the holidays resulting from the ASEAN meetings have prevented them from processing the arrests. The detainees said they have been inside the cell for more than a week.

One female former detainee said her family had to raise P40,000 before she was released after four days. Others were not as lucky as they had to endure the subhuman conditions inside the dark, cramped cell for many days before their families could raise enough to get them out.

It was clear as day that Domingo and his subordinates have violated the Bill of Rights, the Anti-Torture Law (Republic Act 9745), the UN Convention on Torture and the 2013 PNP Operations Manual that requires the immediate documentation of detainees, arrested suspects, and suspects killed in police operations. And yet, De la Rosa still defended the policemen and the Department of Justice has kept silent on the matter.

Duterte promised to look into the matter and said he would call De la Rosa. But on the same day, the PNP chief said his men had nothing wrong. So what do we expect now from the President's promise? Will he ignore De la Rosa's comment and order the DOJ to investigate the matter? Or will he just stand by and let the controversy settle down? Or maybe even divert the people's attention by killing Abu-looking suspects in another tourist resort?

Sen. Panfilo Lacson, a former PNP chief, said De la Rosa's defense of the secret cell was "incomprehensible" and "very arrogant." "Defending policemen for maintaining an unlivable secret prison cell hidden behind a book shelf inside a police station is incomprehensible. It is also very arrogant," he said.

This secret cell incident, the killing of South Korean businessman Jee Ick-joo allegedly after the family's failure to pay the money being demanded by the policemen who were holding him, and the daily murder of drug suspects on the country's streets clearly show that Duterte's brutal drug war had gone on a spiral. Who knows how many more secret cells there are all over the country, or how many more Jee Ick-joos are being held illegally by some unscrupulous policemen while awaiting payment of ransom by their families?

And all De la Rosa could say was that his men had done nothing wrong?

Ooooo

14
There is light at end of the tunnel
April 25, 2017

FINALLY, there are some good news coming from Manila. After months of reading mostly about the brutal and deadly drug war, and curses and threats from a leader who is allergic to criticisms, we are finally hearing what people want from an administration. And it is a good thing that the announcement was made by a group of brilliant and tested economic managers at a forum attended by economic experts. No expletives, no blaming. Just plain facts and figures. Just a promise of better things to come for everybody, including the families of the murdered drug users, who after all are Filipino citizens who deserved the understanding and attention, not just condemnation from their president.

The economic team, which included Finance Secretary Carlos Dominguez III, Economic Planning Secretary Ernesto Pernia and Budget Secretary Benjamin Diokno, presented what Diokno said would usher in a "golden age of infrastructure" in the country.

Following the footsteps of the late strongman, President Ferdinand Marcos, who is obviously the role model of President Duterte, the administration promised to "build, build, build" infrastructure projects worth a total of P3.6 trillion under the so-called TRIP, or three-year rolling infrastructure program from 2018 to 2020.

The three-year promised period is another thing to be awed about. In those years when Presidents had four-year terms, they launched five-year development plans that obviously extend beyond their tenure, a hint that they needed a second term to accomplish the task. Duterte's TRIP promises to finish or at least begin construction of all the big-item projects by 2020, or almost two years before his terms ends in 2022.

Among the big-item projects in the works in that three-year period are the 25-kilometer Mega Manila subway system, the 105-km Mindanao railway system, the 8-km elevated NLEX-SLEX connector road, two bridges across the Pasig River connecting Bonifacio Global City to Ortigas Road and Lawton Avenue, the 38-km PNR railway line between Malolos, Bulacan and Metro Manila, the 69.5-km PNR line between Manila and Clark airport, the 72-km PNR line between Manila and Los Banos, Laguna, the 581-km PNR line between Manila and Legazpi City, the 65-km passenger and cargo rail between Subic and Clark, and a 13,700 sq. m. common station for the three railway lines.

Actually, the Duterte administration plans to spend a total of P8.4 trillion over the next six years that include Congress-approved and appropriated projects inherited from the previous administrations. These projects that remain in the planning stage after many years were 11 projects worth P323 billion under the Aquino administration and one worth P5.44 billion under the Arroyo administration.

Noticeable here was the failure of the administration of President Noynoy Aquino to implement 11 big projects that already had been approved and given appropriation by Congress. The Aquino administration was either too cautious in implementing projects prone to corruption or was simply too incompetent to work on them. In fact, Aquino did not honor a few major public contracts with foreign companies, such as the Laguna Lake and the NAIA 3 Piatco contract, that earned the ire and distrust of foreign investors.

On the other hand, while the Aquino administration was too cautious with regards public works contracts, the Gloria Macapagal Arroyo administration was too lenient in granting contracts that turned out to be laden with corruption.

Another great thing that turned up during the "Dutertenomics Forum," according to some of those who attended, was that instead of the usual tossing of the blame to the previous administration, the new economic managers cited the good work done by the previous administrations for the economic momentum the country has gained through the years. Especially in the previous six years, we had to go through a lot of blaming and chest-beating by the Aquino administration.

Still, we have to welcome this great news with caution. We should all know by now that for decades now, infrastructure projects have always been the biggest source of corruption in the country. It is common knowledge that commissions paid out to government officials ranging from 15 to 30 percent are already marked into bids submitted by contractors, and a few millions more in bribes are given to officials making decisions on the bids. To recover these costs, contractors cut corners resulting in inadequate and substandard projects.

The economic managers said that things would be different this time as President Duterte had repeatedly promised to curb corruption and cut red tape during his term. The economic team also promised to have effective monitoring of all the projects and to get as many projects as possible started on time.

Subways, new railway systems, new bridges and new roads could solve many of our country's problems in transportation and trade, and even help decongest Metro Manila as they would encourage investors to build factories and other businesses outside the overcrowded metropolis and people to go back to the provinces where work would then be available. It can also strongly boost tourism as more places become accessible to both domestic and foreign tourists.

An adequate and reliable infrastructure network has always been the main reason foreign investors have been shying away from the Philippines, and why, despite the recent outstanding growth rate, the country is still lagging behind our ASEAN neighbors. Hopefully, with a decent infrastructure network, as promised by the new economic team, the administration's 10-point socioeconomic agenda would be more attainable and be able to reduce poverty from 21.6 percent in 2015 to 13 to 15 percent by 2022.

We can only hope the politicians would cooperate this time. And that's the other caveat that we have to consider. Congress will have to approve new tax reform measures that would cover most of the costs of these projects and the appropriations for some. And that could be the biggest hurdle the economic managers could face to realize the "golden age of infrastructure."

It would be in Congress, especially in the House of Representatives where appropriations originate, where the negotiations would be held and history tells us that the "golden age of infrastructure" could easily turn into a "golden age of corruption" unless Duterte shows sincerity and a strong political will to pursue his promise of a corruption-free government.

Maybe it's time for Duterte to deviate from his brutal drug war and focus more on the economic side of governance while making sure to curb corruption. After all, he has already made his point to criminals and drug lords, and hopefully to corrupt politicians. He can yet turn his image around and leave a legacy of economic prosperity for all.

Ooooo

15
Stop flying the unfriendly skies
April 15, 2017

MORE THAN a half century after United Airlines launched its famous slogan "Fly the Friendly Skies," the giant airliner has become a paradox on how to treat its passengers properly and in a friendly manner. After the brutal and bloody removal of Vietnamese doctor David Dao, a paying passenger who had confirmed booking and seat, last Monday to accommodate its non-paying flight crew, United can no longer claim the promise to fly its passengers on the friendly skies.

The inhumane treatment of Dao, who was already seated on his confirmed seat beside his wife when asked to vacate the seat and leave the plane, seems to validate a customer satisfaction survey by JD Powers that showed in 2016 that United Airlines, who since its merger with Continental Airlines has become the world's largest airline, has also become one of the world's worst airlines in terms of services. The JD Powers survey showed that only the budget airline Frontier had a worse score than United.

Dao was bodily dragged by Chicago policemen, who had been summoned by United managers to help evict the Vietnamese doctor, resulting in bloodied nose, concussions and lost teeth, according to Dao's lawyers.

Unfortunately for United, passengers now have cellphones that can record such inhuman incidents unlike in 1965, when it first claimed to be the "friendly skies." The videos from some of those cell phones went viral and were seen by millions of potential United passengers all over the world, sparking outrage that were read and seen in social media, in newspapers, on television, on radio and all available media.

United chairman and CEO Oscar Munoz poured oil into the fire when, in an attempt to justify Dao's brutal removal and to control the PR nightmare that the incident has brought about, he wrote in an in-house email that the action was justified because Dao had become "disruptive" and "belligerent" when asked to vacate his seat. The email was leaked, sparking even more outrage and demand for boycott of the airlines.

Nothing can justify the brutality with which United evicted a paying and quietly seated passenger. Even if the passenger had become "belligerent." Who wouldn't be angry if told that he had to vacate the seat that airline check-in personnel had confirmed for him and in which he is seated comfortably waiting for the plane to take off? After all, his ticket had been processed by a ticket agent, checked in by airline personnel, and allowed to sit by the flight attendant to his assigned seat.

Even if airlines are allowed to overbook, they still need to make sure the procedure would be done properly and not to the detriment of paying passengers, that removal is voluntary on the part of the passengers, and it is done before passengers board the plane. Why didn't they ask for volunteers earlier in the pre-boarding area? Why did they have to sacrifice paying passengers in favor of their own non-paying personnel? If the crew needed to be in another airport for another flight, why didn't they just hire a private plane to fly them? Why was the crew not checked in earlier if they needed to take the flight? It seems to me like it was mismanagement or lack of planning on the part of airline executives at the Chicago airport.

The incident has triggered a call from all sectors for the immediate review of the policy that allows airlines to overbook and bump passengers from flights. Overbooking has become common practice among airlines to ensure that no seats would be empty in case some passengers decided in the last minute to cancel their reservation. This is simply corporate greed to the detriment of plane passengers.

United Continental, according to aviation experts, is in the forefront of this vicious practice that has helped them to make a hefty $10-billion profit in the last two years. With that amount, flying that flight crew by private plane would have been just a drop in the bucket and wouldn't even cause a dent on their profitability, but they would rather bodily drag a paying passenger with a confirmed booking and seat.

I'm almost certain Dao was chosen because he was an Asian American. Asians have been stereotyped as a law-abiding and subservient people. United Airlines insists the four passengers that were chosen to be bumped off from the flight were randomly selected. How? By a computer? By drawing lots? Or did the flight attendants select Dao because of his ethnicity?

They probably thought Dao, being an Asian American, would quietly comply with demands for him to vacate his seat and leave the plane. But the 69-year-old doctor said he needed to get home because patients were waiting for him and rightfully decided to resist any attempt to remove him.

Besides, he was already assigned that seat and the plane was about to take off.

"I have to go home! I have to go home! Just kill me. Just kill me," Dao screamed as he was being manhandled by police and airline security.

Who was that very important person that could just take his seat, he probably thought. It turned out, the four seats would be taken by a United Airlines flight crew. Whatever happened to customer first, or customer is always right? So non-paying airline personnel now have priority over paying and confirmed passengers?

Why did they have to call police to forcefully remove Dao when he was not kicking or punching flight attendants? Why didn't they just leave him be and find a more peaceful and humane solution to the problem? Why did they have to treat him like a criminal?

It was not even a case of overbooking because all passengers had their seats. The airline just wanted to fly their four flight crew. It was a simple case of battery and assault, said a lawyer who read the 45-page "contract of carriage."

By his arrogance in refusing to apologize and justifying his employees' action, the United CEO confounded his company's problems. He apologized only after the global outrage went on an uncontrollable spiral and after United stocks fell 1.1 percent at the end of trading day on Monday.

There is no excuse for cruel and inhuman behavior. United must pay the price with hefty punitive and exemplary damages in a legal suit or settlement and must immediately start a review of their overbooking and similar policies.

Or better still, plane passengers can simply avoid flying the unfriendly skies.   Ooooo

16
'The rants of a petty tyrant'
April 7, 2017

IN THE past two weeks, President Duterte and his allies have been kept busy attacking the President's critics, in particular Vice President Leni Robredo, the European Union and the media. If there's anything certain in the Homeland these days, it's that if you criticize the President, you should expect a torrent of curses and counter-attack from the tough-talking Chief Executive, scheming political allies, and trash-talking trolls.

Sen. Leila de Lima, Duterte's fiercest critics, learned this the hard way. Although still able to send press statements from her detention cell, the fiery lady senator has been effectively kept at bay by her incarceration on obviously trumped-up charges.

After releasing a video for presentation to the United Nations criticizing the Duterte administration's brutal and deadly war on illegal drugs, Robredo is now feeling the pressure. Being a respectable and charming lady, she has been spared the expletives from Duterte but must now face an impeachment complaint filed before the House of Representatives, where the administration's super majority hopes to end her Cinderella ascension to the vice presidency.

Duterte supposedly had ordered his allies to stop impeachment moves against her and personally reassured her that the impeachment wouldn't succeed, but all these appeared to be another of his double-talk as very close allies Justice Secretary Vitaliano Aguirre III and House Speaker

Pantaleon Alvarez continued to work for her impeachment, with Aguirre saying Duterte's remark about the impeachment moves against Robredo was just "his personal opinion."

"Impeachment involves the power and discretion of Congress, so it will be a congressional call, not the President's call," Aguirre told reporters. Does he want us to believe that he would make that kind of remark without the permission of his boss? Apparently, Duterte doesn't want to look bad before a charming lady like Robredo but just the same, he would be ready to pull the trigger if the latter makes a wrong move again.

The impeachment complaint was filed by Marcos loyalist Oliver Lozano after being encouraged by Alvarez's remark that Robredo should be impeached for her treasonous act in the UN video. Over the weekend, thousands of loyal Duterte supporters held a "Palit-Bise" (Replace Vice President) rally at the Luneta to press for Robredo's ouster.

If he were civil after Robredo's criticism, Duterte was in his usual kanto-boy manners as he lambasted the European Union for criticizing anew his drug war, threatening to slap the EU's "sons of b****** " politicians.

"Come here and we will talk because I want to slap you," he told the members of the European Parliament which had threatened to withdraw tariff privileges on Philippine exports.

A few days earlier, after the EU Parliament passed a resolution condemning extrajudicial killings in the Philippines and calling on the Philippine government to immediately release De Lima, the President flared: "You madmen, you sons of b******. Stop interfering with us. I would be happy to hang you. If it were up to me I would hang you all."

The worst was yet to come. Obviously pissed by the daily reports on criticisms on extrajudicial killings and other controversial issues that continue to hound his administration, Duterte lashed at the owners of the Philippine Daily Inquirer and the ABS-CBN News, calling them "oligarchs" and "scourges of society."

"Journalism is always antagonistic, but do not put too much slant [in the reports]," Duterte said in his expletive-laden speech in Malacanang. "You smell bad. The Prietos, the Lopezes – you're full of shit," he said. He claimed that media organizations would publish anything they would be paid to publish. "These rich people, you think they're so honest, respected members of society. These sons of bitches are all about money. It's true," he said.

And then he went on as he singled out the Inquirer: "What I'm saying is, they are the ones saying I am killing the poor. Yesterday's Inquirer was really bullshit, son of a bitch. It's really garbage. Even during the elections."

Duterte said he was not scaring the Inquirer, but it would meet its "karma" someday.

"Talagang mga walanghiya ang mga putang-inang journalists na yan (These son-of-a-bitch journalists have no shame)," he fumed. Whew! If that did not sound like a threat, I must be imagining things. Or maybe, the President was just using a "hyperbole," as his spokesman Secretary Emilio Abella says every time his boss explodes into his trash talks like a runaway train.

It does not end there.

"That is the truth, Inquirer: You are bullshit, and also ABS-CBN," he said. "You put out garbage.

Somebody should tell you now, you sons of bitches, you engage in too much foolishness. Somebody should say: 'You son of a bitch." They might be afraid to say it. I will attack, even every day."

"Ulol pala kayo. Mabuti magkababuyan na tayo dito. Eh ano? Di magbabuyan tayo araw-araw (You jerks. We'd be better off smearing each other here. We can do this every day)," he added. And then he threatened to put up his own program on government-owned PTV-4 to launch his attacks against the media. He even threatened to expose the lives of the media owners' children.

Is this the President of the Republic of the Philippines? Is this the leader elected by 16 million Filipinos last year?

As a longtime journalist, I stand side by side with media men in condemning Duterte's rants against the media. The National Union of Journalists of the Philippines reflected the sentiments of self-respecting media members in the country.

"Your incoherent and foul-mouthed rant against two of the country's major media outfits – the Philippine Daily Inquirer and ABS-CBN – was not only unwarranted, it was absolutely twisted," the NUJP said in a statement.

The President was the one who was rude, not the media agencies, NUJP said.

"It was a brazen abuse of your immense power as chief executive of this land and only shows how little, if any, appreciation you have of democracy and governance,"" it said. "It is a mindset of the petty tyrant who mistakenly believes public office is an entitlement that allows you to flaunt the laws of the land that both grant you power and ensure the checks that prevent you from abusing that power," it added.

It also said it would be futile to ask Duterte to apologize or to come to his senses.

But the independent media would not stop doing its job just because of his rants, it said.

"But one thing we can assure you of, Sir, your curses and your threats cannot and will not prevent us, the community of independent Filipino journalists, from fulfilling our duty to inform the people as best we can of what is happening to our country, whether you agree with what we report or not," NUJP said.

Amen.

Ooooo

17
Duterte's latest affront to democracy
March 28, 2017

WHY ARE we not surprised that President Duterte wants the coming barangay elections to be postponed again and that he be allowed to just appoint the more than 344,000 village officials throughout the country?

From the time that it became evident that he was going to be the next President, Duterte has mimicked his self-professed idol, the late dictator Ferdinand Marcos. While Marcos used the communist threat to justify his dictatorial rule, Duterte has been using the drug menace to justify his strongman tendencies, particularly in the thousands of extrajudicial killings since he took office and the stifling of dissent, including the detention of his fiercest critic, Sen. Leila de Lima.

Repeatedly claiming that the country is becoming a narco-state run by narco-politicians, Duterte has made thousands of local officials and policemen cower in fear as he threatened to jail or eliminate officials and policemen engaged in illegal trade or conniving with drug lords.

His henchman in the Department of Justice, Secretary Vitaliano Aguirre III, arrested and detained De Lima on obviously trumped-up charges based solely on the statements of convicted drug lords. The move failed to silence De Lima, who continues to make statements from his cell but the arrest and detention sent a chilling message to other oppositionists and critics that they could suffer the same fate.

Duterte has repeatedly warned that he would abolish Congress and proclaim a revolutionary government if Congress gets in his way to combat crime, especially drug addiction, and corruption in the government. Last Thursday, he warned again that would declare martial law to eradicate illegal drugs and a range of other security threats.

"If I declare martial law, I will finish all the problems, not just drugs," Duterte told reporters after returning from Thailand, which is under military rule. Duterte said that, as part of martial law, he may create military courts to hear cases against terrorists. "I will allow the military to try you and put you to death by hanging," he said, referring to Islamic militants in Mindanao.

But even before he could declare martial law, the Davao strongman wants to control the barangays in the country.

Claiming that 40 percent of barangay officials are involved in the illegal drug trade, the President now wants to appoint all the officials from the 43,000 barangays all over the country instead of allowing the people to elect them. Last year, Duterte signed a law that postponed the barangay elections originally scheduled last October for one full year. With October approaching again, he wants the Local Government Code amended to enable him to do away with the elections and just appoint all the barangay officials.

Marcos used the barangays to perpetuate his hold to power. One year into his martial law rule, Marcos ordered the convening of 35,000 citizens assemblies, later to be known as sangguniang barangay or barangay councils, for purposes of ratifying the 1973 Constitution. From Jan. 10 to 15, 1973, a referendum was held through the citizens' assemblies that posed this question: "Do you want martial law to continue?"

On Jan. 17, 1973, Marcos issued Proclamation No. 1104, which claimed that, based on the results of the referendum in which "15,224,518 voted for the continuation of martial law as against only 843,051 who voted against it," he was now declaring "that martial law shall continue in accordance with the needs of the time and the desire of the Filipino people."

So, will Duterte also use the appointed barangay officials to push the shift to a federal system of government, or maybe even legitimize a martial declaration in case it becomes necessary to eliminate the drug menace and terrorism, as he claims he might do?

Not missing the signal from their boss, Duterte's allies scrambled to make his wish come true. Surigao Del Norte Rep. Robert Ace Barbers filed House Bill 5359 seeking to postpone the 2017 barangay and Sanggunian Kabataan (SK) elections to May 2020, and subsequent elections to May 2023 and three years thereafter and to allow the President to appoint the village officials.

Why postpone the elections every three years and not just abolish the elections altogether? The opinion of election laws expert lawyer Romulo Macalintal may provide the answer. Macalintal said Duterte's plan to appoint all barangay officials nationwide violates the Constitution. He said the 1987 Constitution states that barangay officials, like all other local officials, should be elected.

Indeed, by just postponing the elections and appointing officials in the interim, Duterte may be able to go around the constitutional requirement until the end of his term. Smart but not necessarily constitutionally infirm. Macalintal said the issue would go all the way to the Supreme Court.

Even former Senate President Aquilino Pimentel Jr., the founder of Duterte's party, PDP-Laban, and author of the Local Government Code that created the barangays and instituted the election of barangay officials, rejected the idea.

"If officials are appointed, it will undermine the purpose of the Local Government Code, which is meant to reduce the influence of central government and instead empower the electorate on the barangay level," the elder Pimentel said. Pimentel underscored that the loyalty of appointed officials would generally be to the appointing power. "But if they are not appointed by one person, their loyalty will be with the people who elected them," he said.

Pimentel and others opposed to Duterte's plan said if Duterte were so concerned that 40 percent of barangay officials were tainted with illegal drugs, why not file charges against them to let the people know who among their officials are involved in the illegal drug trade so they can vote against them?

Barangays are the government units that deal directly with the people. They are the embodiment of grassroots democracy and deciding who would administer affairs in the villages should be left in the hands of the people, not to an appointing authority.

But knowing the mentality of Duterte and his allies, they would not listen to their party's elder and go ahead ramming Barbers' bill through the rubber stamp called the House of Representatives. It will be up to the Senate, where many members still rely on their wisdom and conscience, and the Supreme Court to stop this latest affront to democracy and the rule of law under the Duterte administration.

Ooooo

18

Rape on sovereignty: Relax and enjoy it?
March 20, 2017

WHO was it who said about rape that "if it's inevitable, relax and enjoy it?"

This seems to sum up the policy of the Duterte administration with regards to China's bullying in the South China Sea. We can't afford to fight China, so let them do what they want to do in the South China Sea and let's just enjoy the economic benefits it brings.

Over the weekend, after China said it plans to build an environmental monitoring station (read it radar station) on Scarborough Shoal (Panatag Shoal), a hotspot in the ongoing territorial dispute in the South China Sea between the Philippines and China, President Duterte said: "We cannot stop China from doing its thing. Even the Americans were not able to stop them. So what do you want me to do? Declare war against China? I can but we'll lose all our military and policemen tomorrow, and we are a destroyed nation. And we cannot assert even a single sentence of any provision that we signed."

That's a very clear statement of resignation. A defeatist attitude from a guy who has shown an image of toughness throughout his long political career.

Defense Secretary Delfin Lorenzana had earlier said the Americans had stopped the Chinese from reclaiming the highly disputed shoal, but Duterte said no one can stop the Chinese from doing their thing in the South China Sea, not even the Americans. It was the second time in one week that the President had contradicted his defense secretary.

Earlier, after Lorenzana revealed that the government monitored in 2016 a Chinese ship surveying the Benham Rise, a 13 million-hectare undersea region and biodiversity hotspot, Duterte immediately came to the defense of the Chinese, saying China had informed him beforehand of its plan to pass through Benham Rise, an area recognized by the United Nations as part of the Philippines' exclusive economic zone.

The Department of Foreign Affairs had filed a note through Philippine Ambassador to China Chito Sta. Romana, officially asking the Chinese government to explain the presence of one its vessels in Benham Rise, an undersea plateau in the Pacific Ocean west of Luzon that the United Nations on the Limits of the Continental Shelf declared as Philippine waters.

Duterte said the concern of the DFA and the defense department was exaggerated. "Pinalalaki lang yan (it is being exaggerated)," he said. "We don't want to dignify (that). Things are getting great our way. Why spoil it?" he added.

Malacanang said the DFA and DND were informed of the matter beforehand. But both the DFA and the DND denied knowledge of any agreement with China on the presence of the Chinese ship over Benham Rise on UN-declared Philippine waters, which is believed to be rich in natural gas and other mineral resources.

"There are ships through the area exercising freedom of navigation. But the fact that this is within the sovereign rights and jurisdiction of the Philippines any ship would have to get permission from the Philippines if they wish to undertake research," acting Foreign Secretary Enrique Manalo, a career diplomat, said.

The DFA said any exploration or incursion into these waters should be made known to the foreign affairs department and seek the permission of the Philippines. Such a request would have to go through the regular process of informing relevant agencies and negotiation, the DFA spokesman, Undersecretary Charles Jose, said. He said the public deserved to know what was going on inside the government, including the country's relations with other countries.

Twice during the past few days, Duterte downplayed any wrongdoing by the Chinese on Philippine waters, after which Chinese Vice Premier Wang Yang visited Duterte in Davao City and announced that China is ready to help the Philippines build a P218-billion railway that would connect key cities in Mindanao, Duterte's dream project. This followed an earlier offer of $10-billion worth of assistance.

To this offer, Duterte said: "Let me publicly again thank President Xi Jinping and the Chinese people for loving us and giving us enough leeway to survive the rigors of economic life in this planet."

So that's the part where the country was supposed to enjoy the rape of its sovereignty by the Chinese? Things are going our way, as Duterte said, why spoil it? Maybe we should spread our legs some more?

This attitude coming from the President has apparently emboldened China, which only recently said it has extended its maritime jurisdiction to cover all seas "under its jurisdiction."

In July last year, the arbitral court of the UN Convention on the Law of the Sea (UNCLOS) rejected China's nine-dash line that serves as its basis for claiming sovereignty over most of the South China Sea, including the Scarborough Shoal. Last week, China ignored the ruling anew when it arrogantly insisted that it is within their sovereignty what to do what they want to do with Scarborough (Panatag) Shoal.

Obviously concerned about the effects of Duterte's words of affection to the Chinese, Supreme Court Senior Justice Antonio Carpio said the government should avoid actions or statements that express or imply a waived Philippine sovereignty over any of its territories in the South China Sea.

Carpio, who was a member of the country's legal team that argued the Philippine case before the Permanent Court of Arbitration at The Hague and who has been appointed by Duterte as a consultant on South China Sea issues, said that any declaration saying that the country could not stop China from building on Scarborough Shoal actually encouraged the Chinese to build on it.

The eminent justice also reminded the President that as the commander-in-chief, he was tasked by the Constitution to defend the national territory. Although conceding that the country was no match to China militarily, Carpio said this should not deter Duterte from fulfilling his constitutional duty. In the face of the Philippine military disadvantage against China, the least the country could do, he said, was to file a strong protest against Chinese building activities, he said.

Carpio went further by saying that the country should rethink its relations with its giant neighbor to the north following China's announcement that it would build a radar station on Scarborough Shoal. He warned that China's move could escalate militarization in the disputed sea to back its excessive maritime claims in the region. The planned environmental monitoring station on Panatag Shoal, he said, may just be an initial step in a creeping occupation, as seen in previous Chinese incursions at Kagitingan (Fiery Cross) Reef, where the Chinese had built a naval base.

Instead of ignoring these warnings from Carpio and members of his Cabinet, Duterte should stop focusing on the billions of dollars that China is dangling, and start looking further into the future when China has all but encircled the country with military garrisons just miles from its shores and when China has taken away its right to exploit the mineral resources that abound on those reefs and waters, which could be worth a hundred times over what China is offering him now.

That's when the rape would hurt.

Ooooo

19
Where is the change?
March 14, 2017

THERE is not much difference between the previous and current administration as far as dispensing justice is concerned. Former President Aquino was quick to defend his friends and allies amid public protests. And so is President Duterte.

This became apparent last week when President Duterte said he was willing to forget about cigarette maker Mighty Corp.'s use of fake tax stamps as long as the Mighty Corp.'s owner, his long time acquaintance Alex Wongchuking, was willing to pay the government P3 billion to settle his tax obligations.

Earlier, Duterte had ordered the arrest of Wongchuking but for some reason, Justice Secretary Vitaliano Aguirre III did not arrest him when the tobacco tycoon went to his office. The next day, Duterte said he would forget Wongchuking's falsification of tax stamps for P3 billion that the government, he said, would use to build three hospitals in Sulu, Basilan and Manila.

Obviously, he made the offer without consulting his own officials in the Department of Finance, the Bureau of Customs and the Bureau of Internal Revenue. While he was making his P3-billion settlement offer, Finance Secretary Carlos Dominguez was telling reporters that the department has airtight case against Wongchuking for faking tax stamps and would pursue tax evasion and other charges.

Dominguez later told Duterte that the P3-billion tax settlement that he had offered Wongchuking was too small and that the total amount the cigarette maker had in unpaid taxes could be 10 times over the P3-billion offer, after which Duterte said Wongchuking must pay P15 billion.

Still, letting Wongkuching, a fellow mistah in PMA Class '67, scot-free after it had been established that Mighty Corp. faked its own stamps to evade paying billions of taxes is not the kind of justice that people expected from an administration that trumpets its avowal to combat crime and corruption.

After he offered Wongchuking to settle for P3 billion, Duterte even assured that the latter won't be jailed. "Pay double, I'll forget about it. Anyway, I assure him that if someone in power pursues the case, I can always pardon him," he said. It's a complete rebuff of Dominguez, his chief economic adviser, who vowed to pursue tax evasion and falsification charges against Wongchuking.

While what Duterte said that tax evasion, whether done intentionally or unintentionally, may be settled legally could be true, it only settles the monetary part. In this case, where the tax evader was reported to have blatantly falsified tax stamps, Wongchuking should still face criminal charges for not only falsification of public document but, more importantly, for economic sabotage or even plunder, which some of Duterte's allies want to be punished by death.

More than the tax evasion part, Duterte should have taken into consideration findings by the Commission on Audit, the Bureau of Customs and the BIR that the faking of tax stamps has been going on since 2014, and that the falsification would not have been carried out without the connivance of persons involved in the printing of the tax stamps.

For example, it has been established that APO Production Unit Inc., a government entity, was overprinting internal revenue stamps being affixed to cigarette packs as proof that concise taxes have been paid on the product.

The Bureau of Customs report also said that from 2014 to 2016, more than 13.5 million stamps were declared defective, although further investigation showed that the actual number could climb to 37.4 million. The report also found that the QR codes used in these defective and face stamps were reused many times to generate more fake stamps.

The BOC task force also found that Asa Color Trading Corp., which supplies the silver ink being used by APO in the tax stamps' silver strip, incidentally also supplies Mighty's ink and that United Graphic Expression Corp., the contract supplier of base printing of tax stamps to APO, is also Mighty's supplier. Certainly, these companies did not just happen to be the same suppliers for the agency that prints tax stamps and the company found to be printing their own fake stamps.

These fake stamps have cost the government billions of pesos in lost revenues, definitely many times over even the upped P15-billion settlement offer to Wongchuking.

While Aguirre was quick to arrest Sen. Leila de Lima over weak evidence and to justify the killing of thousands of poor people for a minor drug offense, he and his boss Duterte were unwilling to arrest nor file charges against Wongchuking, whose alleged blatant falsification of tax stamps has caused billions of pesos in lost revenue. If this is not economic sabotage or plunder, I don't know what is.

Duterte and Aguirre were willing to give an alleged economic saboteur a second chance but not a poor, small-time drug user. Is Wongchuking more human than those drug addicts, who Aguirre said were not part of humanity?

By letting Wongchuking go scot-free after settling his tax arrears, the government is sending wrong signals to tax evaders and other criminals that it's alright as long as they pay up. That's the government taking bribes and condoning crime and corruption.

Or has the government become so pragmatic in its approach to justice that it was considering clearing convicted Janet Napoles of kidnaping charges, after which Napoles said De Lima tried to extort money from her while being investigated on the pork barrel scam.

But more than a possible witness against Duterte's critic, Wongchuking is a friend of the President. Why should he worry when the President himself said he would pardon him even if someone in power – in this case Dominguez and company – decided to pursue a criminal case?

Which brings us to another incident that was revealed the past week. Sandra Cam berated and cursed a poor airport worker and her manager last month when she was not accorded the VIP treatment she had expected. Cam dropped the name of the President's chief lieutenant, Christopher Go, and even boasted of her anticipated appointment to a Cabinet post in three months. Cam, a former jueteng whistleblower and an avid supporter of Duterte during the presidential campaign, even threatened to have the two helpless airport employees dismissed for not giving her VIP treatment and for charging her P1,200 for the use of the VIP lounge.

And guess how Duterte reacted to Cam's behavior? Duterte said he was willing to offer Cam a government post in return for her help in his campaign and that he was leaving it to the people to judge her.

"She helped me during the last election. I'll be frank. Her behavior? Let the public judge it. She helped me and I will help her. That's a debt of gratitude," Duterte told reporters. "If she would ask for work, I'd give her work. It's not because she was shouting there. That's her business."

What more can I say?

Ooooo

20
'A country where everyone lives in fear'
March 8, 2017

IN MY previous article, I asked, "Will De Lima's arrest rouse the opposition?" I asked this because it has become apparent with the arrest of Sen. Leila de Lima, the President's fiercest critic, on obviously trumped up illegal drug charges that the administration of President Rodrigo Duterte wouldn't tolerate criticisms and opposition to his policies.

The arrest of De Lima was followed by two clear moves to silence the little opposition left to Duterte. The first was the removal of Liberal Party members from key Senate committee chairmanships, and remarks by Solicitor General Jose Calida that charges are being readied against Sen. Antonio Trillanes IV, the other half of the Senate's daring duo.

With the removal of Sen. Franklin Drilon as Senate president pro tempore, and Senators Francis Pangilinan, Bam Aquino and Risa Hontiveros from their committee posts, the key LP leaders were considered out of the majority and became the minority bloc, along with independent Trillanes and the jailed De Lima.

The Duterte administration, which becomes insecure about its hold to power as the weeks wear on, is basically telling the very few left brave enough to criticize the President's policies that coalition members must toe the line or face censure.

The Senate reorganization came after most of the senators, including the LP lawmakers, voted to hear the testimony of retired police officer Arturo Lascañas, who disclosed the other week that he killed people, including radio broadcaster Jun Pala, on orders of Duterte.

In the House of Representatives, the issue where the Duterte allies, led by Speaker Pantaleon Alvarez, wanted all supermajority members to toe the party line is the bill seeking to restore the death penalty. Alvarez fired two deputy speakers – former President Gloria Macapagal Arroyo and Rep. Rolando Andaya – because they opposed the death penalty bill that has been certified as a priority measure by Duterte.

Alvarez warned members of the super majority against blocking the administration-sponsored measure, saying they should resign if they cannot toe the party line. The bullying drove a wedge among coalition members, with LP House leader former Speaker Sonny Belmonte saying the LP would allow members to cast conscience votes.

But political exigency apparently is more important than conscience for a majority of the members of the House of Turncoats, so the death penalty bill still passed on second reading despite the strong objections of some conscientious congressmen.

Nevertheless, the bullying by Duterte's allies in both houses of Congress added fire to the already smoldering rebellious feeling among LP leaders following the arrest of party mate De Lima and the repeated allegations by Duterte and his allies that the LP is plotting against him.

Former President Benigno S. Aquino III, who has so far kept his word to remain silent for at least the first year of the Duterte presidency, said after a party caucus that LP members should "speak up" and let their voices be heard on issues that go against party principles.

But the more telling remark was made by Vice President Leni Robredo, the party chair, who called on his colleagues in the political opposition to toughen up, be braver and be louder in opposing the Duterte administration's policies. She said detaining De Lima sent a "chilling effect" that those who would go against the administration would be penalized.

The fragile-looking Robredo has carried the cudgels for the opposition since the arrest of De Lima. In a scathing speech at the UP School of Economics, Robredo said the Duterte administration has begun to show signs of a creeping dictatorship, beginning with De Lima's detention. It must be noted that De Lima herself had warned early on that the country was on "a slippery slope towards tyranny" under the Duterte administration.

"Some leaders would like us to forget the atrocities of martial law," Robredo said. "Some leaders are too happy to glorify the dictatorship of Marcos, to revise the history so that he is remembered a hero, and not the thief and murderer that he was. Some leaders want to raise the fist of authoritarianism, to sow fear and discord among ourselves, to divide us with lies, violence, and bloodshed," she said. "It has begun."

De Lima's arrest, she said, showed how far the administration would go to stifle opposition.

"So on Friday, the nation woke up to a worrying scene: A senator and a staunch critic of the President was escorted into police custody. The message was loud and clear: Anyone who dares speak dissent is not safe."

Strong words from a lady who remained under the shadow of his popular husband for years, and who reluctantly ran for vice president last year to help boost the candidacy of LP presidential candidate Mar Roxas.

In the first few months of the Duterte presidency, it has been the voices of three ladies – De Lima, Robredo and Chief Justice Maria Lourdes Sereno – that have kept the flames alive for the opposition other than that of Trillanes.

De Lima continues to criticize from her detention cell, but Duterte's hacks in the Department of Justice — Vitaliano Aguirre III — and the Office of the Solicitor General – Jose Calida – want the court to impose a gag order on her, which shouldn't be difficult considering the haste with which the arrest order was issued.

Trillanes accelerated his attacks against Duterte after De Lima's arrest by reviving his allegations that Duterte had P2.2 billion stashed in his bank accounts and by bringing former Davao police officer Arthur Lascanas to the Senate, where the latter alleged that Duterte had personally ordered the killing of criminals and political opponents during his tenure as Davao city mayor.

But these have only made him the next target for silencing. Calida said his office is considering filing charges against the feisty senator for coddling Lascanas and Edgardo Matobato, another Davao Death Squad whistleblower.

The Liberals and other opposition leaders should heed the advice of Aquino and Robredo and step up their opposition to Duterte's questionable policies. Without a strong opposition, Duterte would wield absolute power, and as it has been said, absolute power corrupts absolutely.

Former US President Harry Truman once said: "Once a government is committed to the principle of silencing the voice of opposition, it has only one way to go, and that is down the path of increasingly repressive measures, until it becomes a source of terror to all its citizens and creates a country where everyone lives in fear."

Ooooo

21
Will De Lima's arrest rouse the opposition?
March 5, 2017

IT IS IRONIC that on the day the Filipino people were commemorating the EDSA People Power revolt that restored freedom and democracy in the Philippines, the foremost critic of the present administration would be arrested and detained in an obvious attempt to stifle the opposition and bring back the country to the dark days of the dictatorship.

The arrest of Sen. Leila de Lima, who was the first to warn that the country was on a "slippery slope to tyranny" on the early days of the administration of President Rodrigo Duterte, on obviously trumped up drug charges is a direct threat to all those who would dare cross the path of this administration that they could face the same fate.

"The message was loud and clear: Anyone who dares speak dissent is not safe," Vice President Leni Robredo, who is finally assuming the role of the opposition leader, said it succinctly. "Some leaders want to raise the fist of authoritarianism, to sow fear and discord among ourselves, to divide us with lies, violence, and bloodshed. It has begun."

Indeed, the road to tyranny has begun.

Executive Secretary Salvador Medialdea and Chief Presidential Legal Counsel Salvador Panelo denied political persecution was involved and said that De Lima's arrest merely showed that "the law is enforced regardless of who the subject of a warrant of arrest is, whether the person is holding a high position in government or has an ordinary status in society."

And yet, when two eyewitnesses risked their lives to reveal that the Davao Death Squad did exist and that it was then Mayor Duterte who ordered the killing of hundreds of people in Davao City, including that of radio broadcaster Jun Pala, the Department of Justice wouldn't even lift a finger to investigate their allegations.

Former police officer Arthur Lascanas and self-confessed DDS hit man Edgar Matobato had nothing to gain and everything to lose when they surfaced to tell what they said was the truth, but clearly they are bound to suffer the same fate as other whistleblowers before them did.

And yet, the Department of Justice would rather listen to criminal convicts who stood everything to gain and nothing to lose to tell possibly unsubstantiated lies to pin down De Lima. The conspiracy became evident in the face of leaked reports that Justice Secretary Vitaliano Aguirre II reportedly gave instructions to Bureau of Corrections officials to provide special privileges to the drug lords "in return for the testimony they gave during the congressional inquiry on the proliferation of drugs inside the New Bilibid Prison."

The DOJ lawyers would jail and prosecute a sitting senator and, on the same breath, dismiss illegal drug cases against four known drug lords, including Wu Tuan Yuan alias Peter Co, because they will be utilized as prosecution witnesses against De Lima. The words of notorious drug lords against an elected senator and a former Justice Secretary, and they wouldn't hesitate to take the criminal convicts' words. It's like choosing Barabbas over Jesus Christ to be given freedom and the latter to be crucified.

Malacanang insists the arrest of De Lima on drug charges was not political persecution. But the actions of Aguirre in the rally of Duterte supporters at the Luneta, in what Duterte allies called alternative EDSA celebration, exposed his and the administration's true intention.

"Who do you want to jail next?"
Aguirre posed this question to the crowd gathered at the Quirino Grandstand at the Luneta on Saturday night. "You were saying who you want to jail next? Who?" Aguirre asked again.
The throng shouted back: "Trillanes!" They were referring to Sen. Antonio Trillanes IV, Duterte's other fiercest critic. The smiling justice secretary said: "Okay, help me out then."

The exchange of words between Aguirre and the pro-Duterte crowd all but confirmed that De Lima's arrest was instigated by the administration just as it would now target Trillanes as the next critic to be jailed and silenced. Acting like a triumphant Roman general returning from the Crusade, he seemed to be boasting, "I successfully jailed one critic. Who do you want me to jail next?"

With Aguirre at the helm, it wouldn't be difficult to call his agency the Department of Injustice where one of the bureaus could be called the Bureau of Political Persecution.

Let us not forget that the first act of former President Marcos when he declared martial law was to jail his fiercest critics in Congress and in media, particularly the late Sen. Benigno Aquino Jr. and other opposition senators. At least he declared martial law before silencing them. Duterte's men couldn't wait to declare martial law and instead conspired with criminal convicts to stifle the opposition.

So what will they accuse Trillanes of? It has to be a non-bailable offense. Plunder could be out of the question because the senator wouldn't even touch his pork allocations. Maybe kidnapping or rape, or perhaps another illegal drugs case? Oh, it shouldn't be too difficult to find another one or two convicts willing to lie for freedom or even just leniency.

The arrest of De Lima could boomerang on Duterte as it has many Liberal Party members thinking: "Should we just sit idly as our fellow Liberal is being persecuted by this administration?"

The first sign of a united LP, which should have been the foremost opposition party if not for the political opportunism of many of its elected congressmen, was when leading LP leaders joined Vice President Robredo as he lambasted the Duterte administration in her UP speech. They included Sen. Francis Pangilinan, who also spoke at the forum; House Deputy Speaker Miro Quimbo; Caloocan Rep. Edgar Erice; and former Reps. Erin Tañada and Niel Tupas.

Pangilinan said he found it ironic that on the eve of the 31st anniversary of People Power Revolution, "a critic is being detained." He hinted at the LP's future course of action on De Lima's plight. "In the middle of all this, we need to sit down, talk, engage, discern, and hopefully after discerning, we will act," he said.

Let us not forget that the Liberal Part has a big majority of elected congressmen and senators. If they decide to bolt from the Duterte coalition, the Liberals can do a lot of things that could hurt Duterte, like impeachment. But that's only possible if Duterte does not beat them to the draw with a martial law declaration, as he has always threatened to do.

Ooooo

22
Two damaging testimonies
February 22, 2017

WHEN asked to comment about media killings during a press conference in Davao City a month before his inauguration, President Duterte blurted out expletives and justified the murder of some media men, blaming corruption in the media and irresponsible reporting for the slayings.

"It's not because you're a journalist you're exempted from assassination if you're a son of a bitch," he added. Duterte said the freedom of expression enshrined in the 1987 Constitution would not protect reporters from assassination if they are corrupt or careless in reporting. In essence, he said that corrupt media members were legitimate targets of assassination.

Then, he cited the case of Jun Pala, a radio broadcaster who was murdered in Davao in 2003 while Duterte was mayor. Gunmen on a motorcycle gunned down Pala, who was a vocal critic of Duterte. His murder has never been solved.

"The example here is Pala. I do not want to diminish his memory but he was a rotten son of a bitch. He deserved it," Duterte said.

Now comes former Davao police officer Arthur Lascanas, who admitted on Monday to media men covering the Senate that he was one of three policemen who killed Pala. "Consider the Jun Pala murder case solved. I was one of those who killed Jun Pala," said Lascañas, who said they were paid P3 million plus a P1-million bonus for the kill.

"The first time Mayor Duterte sat as mayor of Davao City, we started what we call salvaging of people, criminal and drug suspects in Davao. We implement the personal orders of Duterte… in all the killings we do in Davao City – whether burying them or throwing them at sea – we're being paid by Mayor Rodrigo Duterte," said Lascanas, who said he was speaking out because he is being bothered by his conscience.

He said policemen and other hit men were paid from P20,000 to P100,000 depending on their targets. The teary-eyed Lascanas even admitted having had his two brothers killed for their alleged involvement in illegal drugs. He said he carried out the killings out of "blind obedience and loyalty" to Duterte.

Lascanas' testimony seemed to give credence to a report earlier this month by Amnesty International that policemen were ordered and paid from P8,000 to P15,000 to carry out executions ordered by their superiors.

Duterte fumed over the AI report. "Why would I give them money just to make them kill people? It's their job. I'm not a weakling president. I'm from Mindanao," he said in Filipino with his usual expletives. Duterte, on the same breath, however, admitted having released about P115 million in intelligence funds to boost the PNP's drug operations dubbed "Oplan Tokhang."

The reaction this time from Malacanang was one of indifference as Communications Secretary Martin Andanar merely dismissed Lascanas' allegations as "all part of a political drama aimed at ousting President Rodrigo Duterte."

Duterte's aides can no longer ignore these accusations. Lascanas' admission corroborated an earlier confession by self-confessed hit man Edgardo Matobato that Duterte personally ordered the killing of several people in Davao, particularly criminal suspects and drug users. At the same time, Lascanas' claim that they were paid to kill seems to back up reports by the Amnesty International that policemen were paid to kill suspected criminals.

At the very least, the Senate should resume its investigation into the Davao Death Squad to shed light on the allegations of both Lascanas and Matobato, who are risking their lives because they said they were bothered by their conscience.

The Senate should also take heed of the suggestion of Sen. Chiz Escudero for the Senate committee on justice and human rights or the committee on public order and dangerous drug to investigate the AI report, saying it is giving the country a bad image.

The Department of Justice, in fact, should reopen investigation of the 13-year unsolved Pala murder case in the wake of Lascanas' allegations to give closure to the family of the slain broadcaster.

More importantly, the allegations by Lascanas and Matobato and the report by Amnesty International cast serious doubts on Duterte's moral ability to lead the nation. If the claims were not true, Malacanang should welcome such an investigation to finally clear the name of the President. The nation cannot move on with its leader himself carrying a heavy burden of doubt on his shoulder.

Andanar cannot continue to claim that Duterte has also been cleared of similar charges in the past in the wake of the damaging testimonies of Lascanas and Matobato. As they say, the truth will set us free.

Ooooo

23
Culture of death
February 17, 2017

I DON'T know what's with this administration, but President Duterte and the men around him seem to believe that to create a better world, those that they deem "criminals and misfits" or not "part of humanity" should be eliminated and sent to hell, if not fed to the sharks on Manila Bay.

When warned by the Amnesty International that the extrajudicial killings of drug dealers and users could constitute crimes against humanity, Justice Secretary Vitaliano Aguirre II — yes the same guy that's under fire for his alleged involvement in the P48-million extortion and bribery at the immigration bureau — asked how can the killings be so when the drugs lords and addicts "are not the humanity."

"How can that be when your war is only against drug lords, drug addicts, drug pushers? You consider them humanity? No. I believe not," he said, echoing his boss's line that these criminals are not human beings, they're animals and deserved to be extinguished from the face of the earth.

Since assuming his post, Duterte has been threatening offenders with death if they did not behave — local officials, gambling lord, erring policemen, yes even tax cheats. Although the President probably didn't mean to really kill them, that he mentions killing as a form of punishment and deterrent is cultivating, slowly but surely, a culture of violence, if not a culture of death, in the country.

And now, he wants to make death for certain offenders legal by restoring the death penalty in the country. House Speaker Pantaleon Alvarez has made it clear that the passage of the death penalty bill is one of the most, if not the most important legislation of this administration, so much so that the President has declared it a priority bill.

Not content with having triggered the killing of more than 7,000 Filipinos – whether by the police or by so-called vigilante groups, it doesn't really matter – in just six months, they now want to make sure those who escaped instant death on the streets by going through the judicial process would get their final retribution in the execution chamber.

Although lethal injection is the preferred way by the few countries that still enforces the death penalty, Duterte would rather do it the old-fashioned brutal way – by public hanging. And mind you the tough-talking Chief Executive would not be satisfied with a single hanging for the really hardened offenders. In May, while waiting to be formally installed as president, Duterte said criminals convicted of murder, robbery and rape should be hanged twice.

"After the first hanging, there will be another ceremony for the second time until the head is completely severed from the body," he said. This is an overkill, of course, often used by Duterte to excite his audience during the presidential campaign. In fact, he even suggested using military snipers to kill criminals.

Again, these were just "hyperboles," as his spokesmen and defenders would say, but we wonder why the leader of a mostly Roman Catholic country would even utter these words.

As has been the case with the brutal drug war, the proposal to restore the death penalty has sorely divided this already fractious nation. And if the administration does not thread carefully on this matter, it could also cause the collapse of his so-called "supermajority" in the House of Representatives that was formed when the political turncoats expectedly gravitated to the party that held the spoils of the war we call presidential elections.

Alvarez, the toughie who was personally handpicked by Duterte to lead the House of Turncoats, has threatened members of the super coalition of severe consequences if they voted against the party stand on the death penalty bill. No, the consequences do not include being shot by a military sniper or being gunned down on the street, but just as severe for a politician who is looking forward to reelection or to a higher office.

Alvarez has warned his fellow PDP-Laban members that they must vote for the restoration of the death penalty or they should leave the party. If they hold committee chairmanships, they would be replaced. To a dyed-in-the-wool politician, this could mean political death – no funding for their pet projects that, in local elections, can spell defeat or victory.

The President believes that restoring the death penalty could be an effective deterrent to crime, just like the public execution by firing squad of the Chinese drug lord at the onset of martial law instilled fear on criminals.

But many believe it was not the fear that they could be next that stopped criminals, but the fear of martial law itself. They argue that if there were no martial law at that time, the execution of Lim Seng would not cause a dent on the crime rate just like the electrocution of four scions of prominent families for the rape of actress Maggie de la Riva just before martial law did not stop other rapists from doing their dastardly crime.

Proponents of the death penalty all over the world cite its role as a major deterrent to crime as the primary reason capital punishments should be imposed. However, such claims have no basis in fact. In the Philippines, for example, according to the late Sen. Joker Arroyo, a longtime human rights lawyer and activist, the revival of the death penalty from 1993 to 2004 did not bring the number of violent crimes down.

In the US, Texas has had the most number of executions for years, but is still ranked 13th in the country in violent crimes and 17th in murders per 100,000 citizens.

The American Civil Liberties Union said there is no credible evidence that the death penalty deters crime more effectively than long terms of imprisonment. The Death Penalty Information

Center, on the other hand, says the murder rate in non-death penalty states has remained consistently lower than the rate in states with the death penalty. In addition, a study published in The Journal of Criminal Law and Criminology found that 88 percent of criminologists in the US believed that the death penalty was not a deterrent to murder.

There is no evidence that serial killers and rapists would consider their death by lethal injection or in the gas chamber prior to committing crimes. Law enforcement experts say criminals usually operate with the belief that they will not be caught.

Proponents also claim that "deserved punishment protects society morally by restoring this just order, making the wrongdoer pay a price equivalent to the harm he has done." Abolitionists, however, counter: "To kill the person who has killed someone close to you is simply to continue the cycle of violence which ultimately destroys the avenger as well as the offender."

The biggest argument against the death penalty, however, especially in the Philippines where the judicial system is far from ideal, is the real possibility that a wrongly convicted person could be put to death for a crime he did not commit but was unable to defend himself in court because of various factors, including inadequate legal representation by court-appointed defense attorneys, serious flaw in police investigative work, racial prejudice, political pressure to solve a case, and misrepresentation of evidence.

It is the poor who can't afford to hire the best lawyers and who often have to rely on public defenders that end up in death rows, unable to defend themselves and nobody willing to listen to their protestation of innocence.

Even in the US, which boasts of one of the best judicial systems in the world, it has been established that two out of three death penalty convictions have been overturned on appeal because of police and prosecutorial misconduct.

Abolitionists suggest that instead of death penalty, those convicted of certain violent crimes should instead be sentenced to life imprisonment without the possibility of parole and made to work while in prison, with a big portion of their pay given to victims or victims' kin as payment of court-ordered restitution.

The death penalty is a barbaric form of state-aided revenge that has long been abolished by civilized society. If restored in the Philippines, it would only boost the culture of death that has begun to prevail over the country.

Ooooo

24
Peace must be patiently pursued
February 7, 2017

AFTER five failed attempts under five presidents at ending the communist insurgency in the Philippines, peace seemed to be within grasp under the Duterte administration. In fact, less than two weeks ago, government peace panel chairman Labor Secretary Silvestre Bello III was so confident of a final peace agreement with the National Democratic Front when he announced in Rome that the peace talks "are breaking new ground and gaining traction towards finally achieving peace in the country."

Bello expected the draft proposals of the two parties to be "initialed" before the third round of the peace talks ended on January 25.

The two sides were discussing the most relevant, yet most contentious, agenda in the talks, which Bello called the "heart and soul" of the peace effort, which is the Comprehensive Agreement on Socio-Economic Reforms (CASER), tackling genuine land reform, national industrialization and the expansion of social services.

No agreement was reached on the government's proposed bilateral ceasefire in Rome, but the two panels were expected to tackle the issue in The Netherlands on Feb. 22-27.

Then last week, things suddenly headed south. First, the military reported that three soldiers were killed by a group of armed men believed to be NPA rebels in Malaybalay City in Bukidnon.

Earlier, the NPA announced that it would lift its ceasefire on Feb. 10 following disagreements on the release of 400 political prisoners while also accusing the government of moving troops into territories it held.

Over the weekend, a few days before NPA's scheduled lifting of its unilateral ceasefire, President Duterte jumped the gun on the insurgents and announced the lifting of the government's six-month unilateral ceasefire. Within hours, Duterte said he was ending the peace talks and ordered government negotiators to come home.

Duterte then ordered the arrest of NDF peace negotiators once they set foot in the country.
"Come home because you're wanted and upon your arrival, I will arrest you and place you back in prison.

If you don't want to go back, you're fugitives. I will cancel your passports and I will inform the international police for an international warrant (for you)," Duterte fumed. He said he now considered the NPA a terrorist group.

Even the negotiating panels of both sides were shocked. They were apparently optimistic they could reach agreement soon on ending the longest active insurgency in the world, which has lasted 45 years.

The shift was swift.

On Monday, soldiers arrested NDF consultant Ariel Arbitrario and a liaison officer, Roderick Munsayac, in Davao City. The Armed Forces of the Philippines resumed its offensive against the rebels while the Philippine National Police announced that it would arrest 12 NDF consultants — couple Benito and Wilma Tiamzon, Vic Ladlad, Afelberto Silva, Alfonso Jazmines, Alfredo Mapano, Loida Magpatoc, Pedro Cudaste, Ruben Salota, Ernesto Lorenzo, Porferio Tuna, Renante Gamara and Tirso Alcantara.

Every president since Cory Aquino tried and failed to reach a peace agreement with the communist rebels. Since then, over 40 rounds of talks have been held but each were stalled by contentious issues on the release of political prisoners and the CPP's inclusion in terrorist lists, not to mention social-political issues. The current talks were also stalled by these same issues.

Both the government and NDF panels expressed hope that the peace talks could continue, especially since they have reached accord on some very difficult issues. But the sides they were representing don't seem to reflect their desire for peace.

While previously giving sympathetic ear to the rebels no other president has ever shown, Duterte's mood suddenly swung to the other extreme, calling his erstwhile friends "terrorists and criminals," and threatening to jail all of them. He showed frustrations over what he deemed unreasonable demand of the NDF to free 400 political prisoners and over the killing of the three soldiers allegedly by the NPA.

"I tried my best to make peace with everybody. These communists, they are spoiled brats. It's as if they are in the government when they make demands," he added. Duterte conceded that he could not fulfill his campaign promise to end the communist rebellion during his six-year term.

The NDF, on the other hand, said the military could have killed the three soldiers to pin the blame on the NPA and to provoke Duterte to call off the peace talks. That is a very serious allegation that the AFP quickly denied.

It is no secret, of course, that the military is wary of any peace negotiation with the rebels and sources are saying that key AFP officers reiterated as much to Duterte during his rounds of military camps. Others are suggesting that Duterte may be fearful of a military coup if he gave in to the rebels' demands, particularly on the release of the 400 political prisoners.

The road to peace that seemed so smooth until about two weeks ago now has become even more difficult to traverse, and the peace that seemed within our grasp suddenly seemingly out of reach.

But both the government and the NDF must not give up hope and do their best to convince Duterte and the rebels in the field to agree to let them pursue peace, however bumpy the road is.

It took four straight years of negotiations between the government of Colombia and the Revolutionary Armed Forces of Colombia (FARC) to end the latter's 52-year insurgency. But in the end, they agreed to call for peace. The Colombian government, the FARC rbels and the people of Colombia were all fatigued by the fighting and they resolved it was time to stop the war and start building peace.

This can happen in the Philippines, too. Everybody has to be patient in pursuing peace and give it a chance.

Ooooo

25
Why I Publish/Reprint Books
Tatay Jobo Elizes
Self-Publisher

Writings are timeless and they act as mirrors to history. I publish writings as they remain relevant anytime. I have seen a lot of good writings in the internet, in magazines and newspapers. But most writers have only one or two articles and therefore not enough material to be published as a book. And yet, many of them need to be published or archived. There are also writers who write a lot but never publish them. There are also old books with no more prints available. The solution is to publish/reprint.

I do this for free because of the print-books-on-demand (POD) system, but the printed or hardcopy is not free

The printed book will always be there among

your collections or libraries. Not all use the internet. The internet access has its technical problems. I can produce fiction, non-fiction, in color also.

My booklist can be seen at http://tinyurl.com/mj76ccq (copy and paste)

Permission had been granted by the author/authors to print their books under my free self-publishing service. They own copyrights to their works.

Interested reader may request free reading of any of my books, articles or essays via online reading or ebook. Just email me.

Thank you.

ooooo